Catching Fireflies

FAMILY NIGHT DEVOTIONAL FUN

Catching Fireflies

FAMILY NIGHT DEVOTIONAL FUN

Marcy Lytle

AMBASSADOR INTERNATIONAL
GREENVILLE, SOUTH CAROLINA & BELFAST, NORTHERN IRELAND

Catching Fireflies
FAMILY NIGHT DEVOTIONAL FUN

© 2007 Marcy Lytle
All rights reserved
Printed in the United States of America

Cover design and Page layout by A&E Media

ISBN 978 1 932307 77 1

Published by the Ambassador Group

Ambassador International
427 Wade Hampton Blvd.
Greenville, SC 29609
USA
www.emeraldhouse.com

and

Ambassador Publications Ltd.
Providence House
Ardenlee Street
Belfast BT6 8QJ
Northern Ireland
www.ambassador-productions.com

The colophon is a trademark of Ambassador

$\mathcal{D}$edication

I would like to thank my parents, Melvin & Rosalee Clearman, for loving me and teaching me to love God with all my heart. A big thanks goes to my sister, Raetta Karnes, for her constant encouragement and support, and to my brother, Bo Clearman, for his love and friendship. Thank you Kendra for the awesome illustrations that made this book come alive! Thank you to Michele Greer, Ginny Hurley and Vivian Douglas for using these studies and giving me a reason to keep writing them. Thank you Jeannie Center for supporting me ever since I wrote the first devotional. Thank you Michell Conner for believing this could be possible. Thank you Jack Hammans for allowing me the oppurtunity to share the devotions with families in the church. A huge thank you to Jon, Kamrin and Conner Lytle for weekly listening to me teach the devotions, giving your critique and finding all of my typos! Thank you Jon for loving me and loving God.

And finally, thank you God for your wonderful creativity and for your words which are life to me. I love getting up early in the morning to hear what new ideas you have to share . . .

Catching Fireflies
FAMILY NIGHT DEVOTIONAL FUN

I remember warm nights in late spring, early summer, waiting for it to get dark outside. When it was just dark enough, my family would go outside and catch fireflies. Fireflies only came out in the dark and it was so fun catching them and watching them glow. Fireflies locate each other by their light, they illuminate the darkness and they warn predators to stay away. Some groups of fireflies even blink in unison throughout the night. I always found the light in these little bugs to be fascinating.

I can't think of a better description for the purpose for this book. Family devotion time should be as fun as catching fireflies. Family devotions should be full of fun activities, because learning about God's love can be fun. Families should be able to locate each other by the light within them, they should illuminate the darkness wherever they are and when families are lit on fire in unison together, they will warn predators like divorce, discord and demise to flee at the sight of the light.

Thus, *Catching Fireflies* is a book of fun, family devotions that uses everyday activities and objects around the house and yard to teach the truths of God's word. It is my desire that every family member catches the fire of God's love and illuminates the world around them, calling others to join in the flight…

This book is for any family or group that desires to learn the truths from the Bible, using things found around the house or yard, to make the lesson fun and practical; something to look forward to each week. Each study is uniquely different and very interactive. There are 52 studies, one for each week of the year, along with a section of special occasion studies to be added in, during the year.

Each study has a "**preparation**" section, which is a list of things needed for the study. Most of the time, these are things found in your closet, your drawers, your kitchen, your yard, etc. There is also a "**how to implement this study**" section to describe how the study will work best.

The studies can be copied and passed out to each person participating, or one person can read the study, assigning participants their parts, as the reader moves through the lesson. All activities for the participants are written in *ITALICS,* so it's easy to tell when an activity is coming up.

I hope you enjoy these studies and enjoy your time together with your friends and family, and most of all, I hope you learn and grow in the love of Jesus Christ and his awesome plan for your life.

TABLE OF CONTENTS:

SEASONAL STUDIES:

Being Poured Out

This study teaches that in order to be used by God, sometimes we have to first be crushed, broken or cut. It is only then that we emit a pleasant fragrance that draws others to Christ.

Preparation: You will need a scented candle, a bottle of perfume, a flower and a small vase, a fresh herb, a piece of gum, a small bag of unopened chips and some fresh bread.

How to implement this study: As you go over each item, discuss how the fragrance gets started, i.e. the candle has to be lit, etc. Talk about how each activity relates to our lives in Christ, and how even though it hurts sometimes, the things we have to go through, God can use our hurts and hard times to make us useful and blessed in his kingdom.

Candle – A scented candle smells nice if you put your nose right up to it, but when it's lit, the fragrance fills the air. Sometimes we wait for others to ask us about Jesus so we can tell them about him, but wouldn't it be nicer if we were *"on fire"* and Jesus filled the room when we walked in. We must be "on fire" for that to happen (*light the candle and smell the fragrance*). ***Read II Corinthians 4:6.***

Perfume – Perfume smells nice in the bottle, but it has to be worn on the individual to take on its special fragrance. Perfume smells a bit different on each individual, as it mixes with the body's chemicals. Jesus wants his goodness and mercy and love to be *"worn"*, so that others will see and be drawn to him. Keeping the perfume bottled up inside may look pretty, but it doesn't serve any purpose. *(Spray the perfume/cologne on each person).* **Read Psalm 23: 4-6.** Even in the presence of enemies, the aroma of Jesus' goodness can fill the air.

Gum – Gum has to be chewed in order to be enjoyed. Does it seem like sometimes life has just *"chewed"* on you, with one thing after the other going wrong? The flavor in gum is brought out the best by chewing. Pray that God will use the bad things that come our way to bring a little flavor to world around us. *(Chew the gum to release the flavor).* **Read James 1:2.**

Flowers – Flowers are beautiful growing in a garden. But if they are to be enjoyed inside, they must be cut and placed in a beautiful vase. Sometimes we don't understand why we have to move from one place to another, but sometimes we have to be *"cut"* out of the garden where we are comfortable and be placed where we will be a blessing to those who admire our beauty, which comes from the Lord *(cut the bottom of the stem and place flower in a vase and let everyone smell it)* **Read Isaiah 61:1-3.**

Herbs – Herbs are best when they are crushed or cooked into a dish. Their flavor enhances the chicken, and fills the room, making all who enter hungry for the food being prepared. Sometimes we may have to be *"crushed"* (humbled) in order to be used by God, but this will bring about much reward if we allow God to use us to bless others *(crush the herb and smell).* **Read Isaiah 53: 10-12.**

Chips – Have you ever opened a new bag of potato chips? You smell the fresh chips and go "aaaahhhh" because it smells so good. Sometimes we try to hide our Christianity so others won't see it. But *"open"* the bag and let others see what's inside! They might just say "aaahhh" and want what you have! (*Smell the fresh chips and enjoy*). **Read Deut. 15: 10, 11.**

FRESH BREAD – Nothing smells better than fresh bread. But bread that is not fresh, smells like mold and is not inviting at all. Sometimes we need to be sure what we are presenting to others is fresh and alive, not old and stale. Let's keep our relationship with Christ fresh so that when we are *"broken"*, the aroma will fill the air... (*Break the bread with each other and smell the freshness*). **Read John 6:48-51.**

On fire   worn   chewed   cut   crushed   open   broken

These don't sound like nice words to describe a Christian, but each one is necessary in our lives in order to be *"poured out"* on others and be a pleasant aroma to the world around us.

BOUND or FREE?

This study discusses the difference between being bound up by sin, pride anger, etc., and how Jesus wants us to be free to enjoy life and enjoy Him.

Preparation: All you need for this bible study is a lot of toilet paper.

How to implement this study: One person will be totally wrapped up in toilet paper, and as they become free, the paper comes off. This represents a person who is bound by sin, getting freedom to live. Have another person already set free, but as he begins to hold grudges, sin, etc., he becomes bound and unable to move. Have someone read the story and scriptures, while the other person acts out the story, following along.

Mummy Fied Finds Freedom

Mr.(or Ms.) Mummy Fied was bound up, basically dead, not able to move or breathe or live. Then he heard *John 3:16* which said that God so loved the world, he gave his only son and whoever believed in him could have eternal life. Mr. Mummy Fied believed and his eyes were opened (*unwrap the head*).

Mr. Mummy Fied decided to find other believers and went to a nice church down the street, where he began to open his heart in love and worship to God (*unwrap torso*). As Mr. Mummy Fied was able to see and hear God now in his life, and his heart was beating steady and strong, he begin to have a desire to give and share his time and money with others.

All of a sudden his arms became free (*unwrap arms*). Mr. Mummy Fied was beginning to see that he began to be blessed as he gave and shared with others. He began to realize that he was nothing without God. He was weak, but God was strong! Mr. Mummy Fied fell to his knees and began a strong prayer time with God (*unwrap legs*).

He began to grow stronger and stronger in his walk with God. What? Yes, Mr. Mummy Fied began to walk and run and share the good news with everyone he met (*unwrap feet*).

Mr. Mummy Fied was free! *Psalm 119:32* became his favorite verse. Every trace of his old self was gone and he was a new man with a new name, Mr. Sett Free!!!!!!

Mr. Proud Luke Takes a Fall

At the same church, there was a man who had been a Christian a long time, Mr. Proud Luke (or Ms. Proud Lucy). He once was set free, but he had slowly let himself become bound up again. *Prov. 16:18* describes Mr. Proud Luke. The first thing Mr. Proud Luke did was quit listening to God and quit caring about others. All he cared about was he himself. So Mr. Proud Luke had let himself get covered up with his selfishness (*cover up the head*).

His head was completely lost in thought about his own

desires. He even quit going to church and worshipping with his friends. He thought he could just make it on his own. His heart began to feel very small and he no longer had room in it for anyone else (*cover up the torso*)

Mr. Proud Luke began to take his money and buy things he didn't need or really want. He just wanted to keep up with his neighbors so they would think he was cool. His hands were no longer open to help anyone else in need (*bind up both hands*).

The next thing he knew, Mr. Proud Luke wasn't even talking to God anymore in prayer. He was just trying to figure everything out on his own. He began to think about how wonderful he was, how he had everything he needed and how he was better than others around him. He wasn't about to bow his knee to anyone! (*Wrap up the legs*).

Mr. Proud Luke became so bound up he didn't realize how he began to look to others. There was no life in him and no one wanted to be around him. He wasn't able to share the good news with anyone because he had become so full of pride (*cover up his feet).* The first part of **Prov. 29:23** describes Mr. Proud Luke. He was not attractive at all.

Mr. Mummy Fied was now Mr. Sett Free, and Mr. Proud Luke was now Mr. Tied Tom.

What is the lesson to be learned from these two stories?

1. Jesus wants us to be free!
2. We need to keep our eyes, ears and heart open to hear God.
3. Our hands must always be open to give.
4. Daily prayer is necessary in order to stay free from worry, fear, etc.

5. Sharing the gospel will set others free!
6. Just as sinners are bound up in sin and need to be set free, Christians can become tangled up in sin, too. We all need to walk in freedom, enjoying God and living for Him.

Read II Corinthians 3: 16-18. Pray for those you know who have not been set free. Pray that you as Christians will walk in freedom and not tangle yourself up with sin and selfishness.

untangle yourself....   *and be set free...*

Clutter

This study teaches us to get rid of all the things in our lives that clutter up our minds and hearts, which then keep us from hear God whisper in our ears.

Preparation: Have a TV, CD and radio prepared to be turned on all at once. Place several items of clothing in a laundry basket, a batch of loose change in a purse, throw some leaves across the table where you will be sitting, pull out a "junk" drawer for display and place two or three bottles of cologne or perfume on the table. Finally, mix cocoa, salt and sour cream together in a bowl, put whip cream and a cherry on top (if you have these available). Provide spoons for all.

How to implement this study: Just follow along below.

(Turn on the radio, TV and CD all at once, fairly loud. Now whisper "You all are so beautiful and lovely to me" very quietly, and notice that the others won't hear because of all the noise).

When we have constant stimulation from TV, music, radio, etc. we are unable to "hear" important things that are said to us. God wants to talk with you daily, whisper his love in your ear, guide your footsteps, sing songs over you, etc. It's pretty hard to hear him say these things if our ears are full of other "stuff" all day long.

READ ZEPHANIAH 3:17.

(Show the laundry basket full of unsorted clothes and ask that someone find an article of clothing that has been hidden at the bottom). Clothes are important and we have to have clothes to wear to be presentable in public. If we wore no clothes, we would be very ashamed and embarrassed. God has clothed us in his righteousness and in his gifts of love, mercy, compassion, etc. However, these "clothes" that we wear need to be taken care of. When we go out to the world, we must be clothed so that we show the world Jesus.

READ ISAIAH 61:10.

If we never pray, never read God's word (things which keep our "clothes" presentable), we will spend unnecessary time hunting for the rights words to say, stumbling around in our walk with God. Finding that perfect shirt to wear is much easier if clothes are sorted and put away where they belong. Finding the right word to say to someone is much easier if we are filing away God's word, hiding it in our hearts.

(Dump out the contents of the coin purse onto the table). Unsorted, saved up change can become heavy and a problem. Unsorted money that we receive can become a problem, as well. When we have loose change or receive money for gifts, or for chores, we shouldn't just throw it in a bag or wallet somewhere, or lay it around the room to be discovered when we clean. Sort your money. Save part of it, give part of it, spend part of it. Keep your blessings organized and ready for use at any time. *(Sort the money, count it and place it aside to give.)*

READ PROVERBS. 10:22.

(Place the plate on the table. Give each person a bite.) Does it taste pretty bad? That's because it's a mixed up bunch of food all thrown together. The foods that were mixed to make this "dessert" are foods that don't belong together. The result is a bad taste. If the foods had been mixed with other ingredients that compliment the taste, the result would have been very tasty. For example, there is cocoa in the bite you took, which tastes very good mixed with sugar and milk. But it tastes very bad with salt and sour cream! Did you know that God's word is "tasty"? When mixed with faith and worship, it makes a very nice treat! But God's word mixed with unbelief, and when read just like it's a "chore", makes it undesirable and something we try to avoid. Ask God to increase your faith. Spend time worshipping Him when you read his word. Taste and see that the Lord is good!

READ JAMES 1:5-8.

(Throw out the leaves across the table). Leaves are so pretty when they fall, and a big pile is so fun to play in! However, leaves left to themselves will get blown about and cover up a beautiful yard, and eventually could cause harm to the grass if left there. Leaves represent the old, which falls off in the winter, in order to make room for the new leaves that will grow back in the spring. God is always at work in us, and as we walk with Him, old habits should begin to die off (lying, cheating, gossiping, etc.) However, we must not just let the old habits sit around waiting to be blown across our path again. Rake them up! Discard them! Thrown them away! Let God completely clean your heart so that the new you can begin to grow (love, joy and peace). *(Clean up the leaves.)*

READ II CORINTHIANS 5:17.

(*Show the "junk" drawer*). This is the drawer in the house where "junk" gets thrown. It usually has all sorts of odd and ends that we think we might need some day. And it is usually the drawer we hope no guests in our house ever see. Do you have a hidden "junk drawer" in your heart? Is there a place where you hide anger at someone, hurt at a friend, an evil thought of some kind? When the junk drawer gets too full it needs to be cleaned out. If you let this hidden spot in your heart where you hide bad feelings get full, you will be a sad, heavy person. Ask God to show you the "junk" you hide, and ask him to clean it out. (*Throw away some junk*).

READ MATTHEW. 11:28-30.

(*Pass around the fragrances so they can be enjoyed.*) Ahhh, thank God for the sense of smell. Nothing smells better than cookies baking in the oven when you're hungry. The scent of hair that has been just washed is so refreshing. A nice fragrant candle can fill a room with an inviting aroma. (Now strike a match and blow it out.) Wow, that just took away every nice smell and all we smell now is the scent of a blown out match. There are some scents like that, which dominate a room and eliminate all the nice fragrances. In a group of friends, where everyone is enjoying the sweet "fragrance" of friendship, an unkind word can bring a foul odor to the room. In a church service, where people are worshiping and enjoying the "aroma" of fellowship with God, a disinterested person who is talking or passing notes can make a "stink" to those around them.

READ ROMANS 12:1-2.

Let's pray together. *(Have someone read the lines and everyone else repeat.)*

Lord, we don't want clutter in our hearts and lives.
We want to hear you above all the noise.
We want our mouths to be filled with choice words.
We want to be good stewards of our money.
We want to hear you whisper in our ear.
We want to get rid of old habits.
We want to get rid of hidden "junk" in our hearts.
And Lord, we want to enjoy the sweet fragrance of fellowship with you!

Come and Dine

This study invites all to come and have "dinner" with Jesus.

Preparation: This study is to be read around the dinner table. Make the dinner a "presentation", with formal setting, music in the background, candles burning and a colorful array of food. Try to include one dish that is new to everyone eating.

How to implement this study: As you eat dinner together, read through the study and respond. After you are finished eating, read the scriptures and discuss.

Give thanks

Do you ever wonder why Jesus gave thanks before he ate? Why do we stop to give thanks before we eat? Food is a basic need we have, and we depend on God for our food, to send the rain and the sun, so that the food is plentiful. Stopping to give thanks reminds us that all good gifts come from above, and we should always be mindful of who gives us those gifts.

Try reciting the first prayer of grace, then for fun recite and act out the second one.

Dear Lord, thank you for this food.
Bless the hands that made it.
Bless it to our use and use us for your service.
And make us ever thoughtful of the needs of others.
Through Christ our Lord we pray. Amen.

God Bless us (hands on shoulders)
God Bless the food (hands around plate)
Amen (hands folded)

Eat what is set before you

The person preparing the meal has spent time, money and energy preparing a meal for the ones he/she loves. There may be something you don't particularly like set before you. However, you can be gracious and receive what is given to you, and politely try something new. You might be surprised and like it, or it may be the worst thing you've ever tasted. However, if you graciously accept the presentation of the meal before you, it will bless your soul and bless the hands of the one who made it.

Try a bite of something new

Use all your senses to enjoy your meal.

Look at the food on the table. Notice the colors of the food. Smell the aromas of the food on the table. Listen to the background music. Now use your hands to pass the food around the table to fill your plate. Finally, taste the food and enjoy your meal together.

Take time to "sense" your meal.

Eat slowly.

A meal should be eaten slowly, chewing each bite, allowing all the flavors to be tasted, and nothing should be hurried. It took a long while for the cook to prepare the meal. Taking time to enjoy each bite, slowing down to use your senses, and conversing with each other make a very enjoyable meal.

Did you know that eating slowly helps with digestion, helps you to not overeat and even helps prevent heart problems?

Try putting your fork down between each bite and don't reload your fork until you have completely chewed and swallowed your previous bite. It's hard, isn't it?

Converse

Mealtime together should be pleasant. It is not a time to argue or fight. Take time to find out what others have to say. Use your listening skills when others are talking. When it's your turn to talk, don't dominate the conversation. Be sure to let everyone talk.

Use these questions to get you started:

Tell us something you learned today.....What was the best thing that happened to you today?....If you had to eat only one thing for a whole week, what would it be?....What's your favorite season and why?

Don't leave until you are satisfied.

Enjoying your meal also means eating until you are satisfied. Don't leave the table hungry or thirsty. This does not mean you need to fill your stomach until you hurt. It does mean that when the table is set with so many good things to eat, there's not a reason to get up until your hunger is gone. Don't go away thirsty when there is something good to drink.

(Ask if you can pass anyone anything else to eat or drink.)

Use your napkin often.

The napkin is there to wipe your hands and face clean as often as you need it. It's okay if you get the napkin dirty. Eating is messy business sometimes and you need to make sure you keep yourself clean. If you spill something, a napkin is necessary to clean it up. A fresh clean napkin should always be part of a nicely set table.

(Wipe your face and hands.)

Now that the meal is over, let's have our final conversation. Did you know that Jesus sets a table before you with good things to eat, daily? Giving thanks, using your senses to enjoy his word and his presence, conversing back and forth with him about your day and your needs, and taking time to enjoy his friendship are all part of dining out with Jesus. He offers forgiveness like a napkin, to wipe your heart clean, if you just ask him. It's available at every meal. The drink he offers will satisfy, so that he fills your heart with joy and peace. As you live your life every day, using your spiritual energy to bless others and bring glory to God, he knows you get hungry and thirsty for another meal with Him, and he gladly sets it before you. All you have to do is pull up a chair and eat.

Jesus ate with sinners. *Read Matthew 9:9-12.* Eating with others is good way to get to know each other and make others feel comfortable. Jesus always shared what he had and it satisfied those who ate. *Read Matthew 14:15-20.* Jesus had compassion on those who were hungry. *Read Matthew 15:32-37.* Jesus prepares a table for us, even in the presence of our enemies. *Read Psalm 23:5.* Wow, what a friend he is. Jesus is ready to eat with us, any time. *Read Rev. 3:20.* Jesus has a table spread for us for all eternity. *Read Rev. 19:9*

Come and dine with Jesus…he has the table set…he will be there to eat and talk with you…

COVERINGS

This study shows how we can be covered and protected in God's love.

Preparation: You will need a big blanket, lid to a pot, a hat, a book cover, sunglasses, a large shirt, concealer (makeup), a bandaid and an umbrella.

How to implement this study: Spread out the blanket and have everyone sit on it, with the other items in the middle. Before you begin, ask if anyone can tell what all of the items have in common (they cover things). Let each person take turns picking up the item and putting it on, or using it. Place each item to the side as you read the verses. Before the last verse, take the entire blanket and have everyone cover up with it.

Read Eph. 4:26,27 A lid on a pot helps keep the steam in, and keeps things from boiling over. We must be careful to keep our anger from boiling over, thus hurting someone.

(As each one passes around the lid, placing it on their head, have them say "Jesus, please keep a lid on my anger.")

Read Mark 4:40,41 A hat protects our head from the wind. Jesus is in control of the winds that blow our way.

(Toss the hat to each other, thanking Jesus for controlling the "winds" in our life.)

Read Colossians 3:1-4 A book cover protects the book from getting dirty. Your old life is "hidden" in Christ and if you keep your mind and heart on him, you will keep yourself from becoming "dirty" from the world around you.

(Pass around the book around and state, "I will cover my ears and eyes from listening to or looking at thing I know will hurt my heart.")

Read Psalm 32:7 Sunglasses protect our eyes from the glare of the sun. He is our hiding place and protects us from trouble.

(Take turns wearing the sunglasses and smiling at one another.)

Read II Cor. 5:1-5 A shirt covers our body, covers our nakedness. We are clothed in righteousness because of Jesus.

(Toss around the shirt and shout thanks Jesus for clothing us in righteousness.)

Read Prov. 10:12 Make-up can hide or conceal our blemishes or marks on our face. Christ's love in shedding his blood covers all our wrongs.

(Let each one rub a speck of concealer on the person next to them, stating that Jesus loves them and blots out all their sins.)

Read Isaiah 53:5 A bandaid covers up a wound so it can heal. Jesus was wounded for us, so our wounds would be healed.

(Place the bandaid in the center of the group and pray together for anyone who is hurting.)

Read Psalm 91:4 An umbrella keeps up from getting soaked in the rain. We can be safe from the rain (hard times) under God's wings (his faithfulness).

(Open the umbrella in the middle of the circle, and all lay on stomachs with heads under the umbrella.)

Read Psalm 17:8,9 A blanket covers us up and makes us feel warm, when the weather is cold. We are the apple of His eye and that should make us feel warm and cozy all the time.

(Place all items aside, and have everyone cover up and say prayers of thanksgiving for the way He covers us).

Diary of the Two Cups

This study contrasts the lives of two "cups", one who is unselfish and loving, and one who is selfish and dry.

Preparation: You will need two large cups or mugs, and a pitcher of water. You will also need a pinch or two of dirt, and a stick.

How to implement this study: The story is about two cups. One cup keeps drawing from the pitcher of water (Jesus) and is always full and ready to be poured out. The other cup is always thinking of herself, thus dry and useful for nothing. As you move through the diary, reading the scriptures and the story, following the directions in the parentheses.

Sunday:

Caring Cup got up and went to church. He worshipped and really enjoyed class.

(pour the cup half full)

Clueless Cup slept til noon, she watched a little TV and stayed inside.

(leave her cup dry)

Monday:

Caring Cup went to school, came home and did homework, read a few scriptures about love. It made his heart feel good. He read *Psalm 23.*

(pour in more water)

Clueless Cup went to school, came home and did some homework and fell asleep early. She was so tired from all the TV she watched on Sunday.

(leave her cup dry)

Tuesday:

Caring Cup went to school, came home and played outside with his friends. That night he prayed for the friends he played with.

(pour a little water back in the pitcher)

Clueless Cup went to school, came home and played with her friends and went to bed mad at the one who accidentally hit her with a ball.

(turn her cup upside down)

Wednesday:

Caring Cup went to school, came home and did some chores his mom asked him to do. He listened to a CD that really blessed his heart. He recalled *Col. 3:20*

(pour a little water in the pitcher, then pour more water back into the cup)

Clueless Cup went to school, came home and stuffed her clothes under her bed and listened to music that really rocked. Some of the words were questionable, but she tried to ignore those.

(turn the cup back over and sprinkle a little dirt inside)

Thursday:

Caring Cup went to school, came home and went to his soccer practice. One of his friends got hurt and he told him he would pray for him. When he got home, he did. He remembered *Matt. 10:8.*

(pour a little water into the pitcher)

Clueless Cup went to school, came home and went to soccer practice. One of her friends got hurt, but Clueless didn't notice because she was hot and thirsty. A friend tried to give her a drink, but she ran off.

(sprinkle very little water into her cup, just enough to make the dirt stick to the sides)

Friday:

Caring Cup went to school, came home and spent some time with his little sister, playing dress-up. This made his little sister happy. He recalled *Luke 6:38.*

(pour a little water into the pitcher)

Clueless Cup went to school, came home and spent some time pestering her little brother. This made him cry.

(sprinkle a little more dirt inside)

Saturday:

Caring Cup was so glad he had a day off. He decided to see what he could do to help his dad. They spent some time helping a neighbor fix his flat tire. He had read *II Cor. 9:6-8* the night before.

(pour most of the water left in the cup back into the pitcher)

Clueless Cup was so glad she had a day off. She decided to see what she could do to annoy her dad. They spent most of the day arguing.

(scrape the dirt around in the glass with a stick)

At the end of the week, Caring Cup was pretty dry. But he knew he would get filled again on Sunday or when he spent some time with Jesus.

At the end of the week, Clueless Cup was dry and dirty. She didn't feel good about her choices...the phone rang...

Caring Cup called Clueless Cup and invited her to come to church on Sunday. Clueless Cup said yes. Clueless Cup also said yes to God.

(pour water from the pitcher into Clueless Cup, swish, and pour it back into the pitcher, leaving the cup clean).

Let Jesus (the living water) pour into your life, so you can be poured out on others.

Dry Bones

This study teaches how people who appear to be dead can be brought back to life.

Preparation: You will need several types of pasta and two dry beans for each person. Place them in a bowl and this will be each person's "valley of dry bones". Use whatever pasta you have, and experiment, making a skeleton out of the pasta: (elbow macaroni for ribs, wagon wheel for head, tubes for collar bones, spirals for leg and arm bones, shells for kneecaps, spaghetti for fingers and toes, lima beans or peanut halves for hip bones). Finally, each one will need a black piece of construction paper, an index card, a pen and glue.

How to implement this study: Hand out the materials listed above and follow directions in parentheses.

READ EZEKIEL 37:1-14

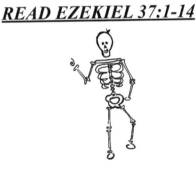

Read verses 1-3 again. (Give each one their valley of dry bones).

These bones represent those around us who are hopeless, dry and dead: the ones in prison, those starving in Africa, the outcast who gets ignored, the abused children and the forgotten elderly. Who else can you think of that would be in this valley?

(As you name other hopeless groups of people, hold up a different bone out of your bowl). (Write down the names of five people groups that were mentioned, on your index card).

Read the following aloud, together:

God has placed us in a world full of dry bones. Can these bones lives? O Lord, you alone know.

Read verses 4-7 again.

As you place glue on each piece, take turns saying out loud, "Dry bones, *(insert here one of the groups you mentioned above)*, hear the word of the Lord. I will make breath enter you and you will come to life."

(Glue the head (wagon wheel), neck and arms (spirals) and fingers (spaghetti) on your paper.

Read verses 8-10 again.

As you place glue on each piece, take turns saying out loud, "Come Lord, breathe into these dead bones, *(insert here a group name)* that they may live."

(Assemble torso of skeleton, by *gluing the ribs (elbow macaroni) and hip bones (lima beans) onto the paper.*

Read verses 11-14 again.

Even though these verses are speaking of Israel as a nation, because of Christ, we too are God's people. It's because of Jesus that we have received the "breath of life". *As you assemble the legs and feet,* take turns saying aloud, "Come Holy Spirit to *(insert a group name)* and bring them out of their hopelessness, breathe life into their souls and give them strength to stand."

(Glue the legs (spirals and shells) and feet (spaghetti) onto the paper.)

Does this look impossible, to see a skeleton of dry, dead bones get up and dance?
Jesus is all about giving life to those who are hopeless, those without life, those without a chance...

(Glue the index card at the bottom of your skeleton or glue it to the edge and let it hang from the bottom.)

As you look at this picture throughout the week, remember to pray for the "dry" bones to receive the life that Jesus gives.

Eggsactly

This study helps us understand people around us and how they are different.

Preparation: You will need seven eggs, cooked different ways, for this lesson. Over-easy (both sides cooked lightly), sunny-side-up (cooked on one side only), scrambled (beaten with milk and stir while cooking), omelet (beaten with water, then cooked and folded over neatly), hard-boiled (cooked in very hot water til solid), poached (cooked in simmering water) and a raw egg. You can get family participation in making them or just have them made ahead of time, arranged on plates for display and taste, if desired (along with a side of toast).

How to implement this study: Eggs represent life. And eggs can be presented in lots of different ways. This study helps us understand our friends around us and "eggsactly" why they may act the way they do. We want to help these friends (and ourselves) to feel loved and special in God's eyes. Follow along below and discuss:

Have you ever had a friend who is cheerful sometimes, and then mean at other times? Some may call them two-faced. We will call this kind of person a sunny-side-up kind of friend.

A sunny-side-up egg is only cooked on one side.

(Have each one choose the sunny-side-up egg, and taste, if they want).

This friend may try to "act" cheerful when they're around certain people, but their "uncooked" side, or mean side, shows up around others. *(Pray for any friends who fit this "eggsact" description.)*

Some of your friends may be like scrambled eggs, stirred up and crazy all the time. Sometimes you wonder, "Who is this person?" because they have so much energy and they're sometimes obnoxious.

(Taste the scrambled eggs.)

These friends we will call scrambled up, sometimes hardly recognizable. *(Pray for any friends who fit this "eggsact" description.)*

Maybe you have friends who are easily offended, it seems like they get mad at the least little thing. They are "overly sensitive", like over-easy eggs. These type eggs are cooked lightly on both sides.

(Taste the over-easy eggs.)

No matter how careful you are around some people, they are still offended. *(If you know someone "eggsactly" like that, pray for them.)*

Omelets are eggs that have been beaten and folded with extra ingredients inside. These are folded into half neatly and are presented nicely on a plate. This will represent the friends who look "cool" and seem to have it all together.

(Taste the omelet.)

These people seem to have lots of friends around them and may be very popular at school. But they need prayer too, because what you see on the outside is not always the same on the inside. *(Pray for the friends who appear to be eggsactly "perfect".)*

Hard boiled eggs are cooked in boiling water until the inside is solid. The shell has to be broken open to get to the egg inside. There are some people who have a hard shell on the outside, but they're really tender inside.

(Taste the hard boiled egg.)

These are usually friends who have had a hard life, maybe someone close to them died or they had to move away and leave all their friends. They may appear to be quiet and may be hard to get to know, but it just might be worth the effort! *(Pray for those friends that fit this "eggsact" description.)*

Raw eggs are runny and gooey. They haven't been cooked yet and really have no shape at all, and definitely don't taste good! These eggs represent friends who are constantly trying to fit in with whoever they are with at the time.

(Just look at the raw egg...don't taste!)

They are always trying to impress others or be someone they're not. They have no place or identity of their own. They may be just the "eggsact" friend you could invite to church sometime. *(Think of someone like this and consider an invitation.)*

The last type of egg we will mention is the poached egg, one that is cooked in simmering water, not too hot, not too cool. Poached eggs are usually not served alone, but with toast or on an English muffin.

(Taste the poached egg with the bread.)

This will represent the friend who always feels left out or stands off to one side, when there's a group of people around. They need to be shown God's "eggsact" love by reaching out to them as a friend. *(Think of someone like this and consider being their friend.)*

Finally, maybe during this study you realized you are like one of these eggs, sometimes nice and sometimes mean, overly sensitive and always getting your feelings hurt, running around crazy all the time, appearing to have it all together and "cool", hurting deep inside and pushing others away, always feeling left out, or maybe just never fitting in anywhere.

Read Psalm 139: 13-18.

God created and formed us in a wonderful, special way. Pray for each other that your life would be "eggsactly" what God intended it to be, full of wonderful things from the hand of God. He is in control of your life and is always forming you to be like him, with his loving hands...

EMOTIONAL SYMPHONY

This study demonstrates the different emotions we all experience and how beautiful they can be, when conducted by God.

Preparation: Make cards or pieces of paper with the listed emotions written on them. Assign each person an emotion or two by pinning their emotion to their shirt. This way, the "conductor" will know who to point to, when the symphony begins. Give the conductor a stick (a real stick or a pointer or drum stick, whatever you have).

How to implement this study: After reading through the study and having each emotion expressed, choose one person to read the passage at the end and "conduct" the symphony of emotions, having each person outwardly express their emotion when the conductor points at them.

Symphony: A pleasing agreement or harmony of several elements.

We are humans and humans are emotional. All of our emotions can either be the downfall of our existence or create a beautiful symphony full of harmony and music, pleasing and beautiful to all who see and hear.

Read Matthew 28:1-8. Notice these women were afraid, but filled with great joy, all at one time. *Read Isaiah 53:3-5* Jesus took our sorrows so we could have peace. One sorrowful experience brought about peace for someone else. *Read on in verses 11-12* about how through the suffering of his soul he experienced satisfaction (contentment), knowing the outcome of his suffering. *Hebrews 12:28* says we should worship God in awe.

There are too many verses to read them all, but all throughout the Bible, we read about the emotions of man, and the emotions of Jesus.

Sometimes if a person is described as being "emotional", we think they are always crying or depressed. However, we are emotional beings and being "emotional" can mean just the opposite of depression. It can mean that we are moved in many ways, to tears, to leaping, to resting, to smiling and even sometimes to running, in reaction to the word of God, the things around us or to things we see and hear. We can allow ourselves to be moved in our emotions towards a deeper walk with Jesus or to loneliness and despair. Our emotions can make horrible sounds to those around us, or be a symphony of harmony and pleasure, resulting in a melodious masterpiece of music.

As you describe each emotion listed below, let the person with that emotion try expressing it in the different ways listed.

Joy is sometime expressed in laughter, jumping up and down, singing or just smiling really big.

Peace is sometimes expressed through a contented smile, comes through reading the word of God or sometimes peace is just the absence of war.

Sorrow can result from a broken heart or a great disappointment, and results in the head hanging low and often great shedding of tears.

Agony comes after a great defeat, after enduring great pain or persevering through a great hardship, often expressing itself in collapse of the body, or an expression of hurt and despair on the face.

<u>Contentment</u> results from having a full stomach and all your needs met, causes you to be able to rest completely and bloom profusely.

<u>Awe</u> can make us stare in wonder, gaze at beauty or fall down in worship.

<u>Fear</u> can make our eyes pop, cause us to run away from danger or hide from others, barely showing our face.

<u>Joy, peace, sorrow, agony, contentment, awe and fear</u> are all emotions each of us experience, sometimes all in one day.

Have the conductor take his stick and have him read the following aloud as he points at the emotions in bold. When he points at the person with that emotion, that person should express that emotion in one of the many ways we mentioned above.
Read slowly and conduct the "symphony of emotions"...

There is great **JOY** in the presence of the Lord. When his presence fills the room, **JOY** is abundant. When we worship our God and stand in **AWE** at his might and power, **PEACE** and **JOY** fill our hearts. We don't have to **FEAR** our enemy, because the **AWE**some God we serve is in control of our lives. Even when we experience the

AGONY of defeat in some of our daily battles, **PEACE** can still rule in our hearts, because the Prince of **PEACE** lives there.

Just look at the face of a baby sleeping so **CONTENTEDLY,** knowing his needs are taken care of. He has no **FEAR** because he knows he will be fed and he knows he is loved. **CONTENTMENT** also comes from knowing who we are and why we are here. Even if we experience great **SORROW** in our lives, we know that **JOY** comes in the morning. Even if we experience great **FEAR** in a dangerous situation, we know that we can ask for **PEACE** to come, and then we can stand in **AWE** as our mighty God delivers us from danger.

Our Lord Jesus was in great **AGONY** when he died on the cross, full of **SORROW** for the sins that he bore. However, he experienced great **JOY** and **PEACE** in knowing he was obeying the will of his Father and that even through death he would come to life. Those who arrived at the tomb were **AWE**struck when they saw that Jesus was not there. They were also full of **FEAR** when they saw the angel, until they received **PEACE** at the angels words stating Jesus had risen indeed. Great **JOY** filled their hearts.

We are humans, and all in one day we might begin with **JOY**ful worship in the morning and hear news that makes us **SORROW**ful later in the day. However, because Jesus lives in our hearts, his abiding **PEACE** sustains us. In the afternoon, we may lose a game and suffer great **AGONY** over it, but when we're driving home we see a rainbow and stand in **AWE** of the beauty God has created. We may start to go to sleep and **FEAR**ful thoughts begin to nag at our minds, but that abiding **PEACE** overrules and we fall asleep with a countenance of **CONTENTMENT**, knowing all is well. **JOY, SORROW, PEACE, AGONY, AWE, FEAR AND CONTENTMENT**: an emotional symphony of harmony to the ears of our God who wonderfully created the emotions of our souls.

ENJOY LIFE!

This study gets us to enjoy laughter and the "sweet" things in life.

Preparation: You will need one candy bar of each of the following: Snicker bar, Milky Way, M&M's, Take 5, Baby Ruth, Skittles, Pay Day and Junior Mints. Cut them into small pieces and give each one a plate or bowl with a piece of each candy bar, and a glass of cold milk. Lay out the wrappers on a table so the participants can see the names to choose. (For an older group, hide the wrappers until they've tried to fill in the blanks). Provide each person with a copy of the study, and a pen or pencil. (*hint*: the words fit into the blanks in the same order as listed above in this paragraph, but perhaps without an "s" in a few places.)

How to implement this study: As you read the story below, a name of each candy bar will fit in the blanks. Find the correct name and eat that piece of candy and enjoy your glass of milk. The purpose of this study is to enjoy your snack and learn a lesson all at the same time! Learning about God and his ways can be fun and enjoyable, and it should be!

Sam and Ryan were sitting with a group of friends at church, along with Beth and Katy and some other kids. Sam began to _____. He couldn't help it, he just felt like laughing. He felt happy and loved his group of friends and that made him smile. Pretty soon, the other kids began to laugh and giggle with him, and the whole group was smiling and laughing.

A new kid, John, was amazed at the joy on these kids' faces. Worship time was about to begin and all the kids stood up to sing. They began singing about the wonders of God and how he made the _____ _____ and all of nature, sea and sky. Most of the kids really seemed to mean what they were singing, John thought. John had never heard the song before, but Ryan was standing near him and John enjoyed listening to him sing. It made John want to know the God they were singing about.

John noticed a poster on the wall that read: **Psalm 92:4 I sing for joy at the works of your hands.**

The next song the band began to play talked about the ___ajestic and ___arvelous God who is wonderful, good and kind. John had never heard such beautiful music. His heart began to ache to know the God they were worshiping. He saw Beth and Katy close their eyes and raise their hands as if they were experiencing something awesome and deep.

After the worship time, the kids sat down in a circle on the floor and just listened to a couple of songs. The leader then instructed everyone to _____ _____, come back together after the break, and they would have a lesson. All of the kids stood up and stretched, and three kids came over to introduce themselves to John. They seemed genuinely excited to have him there, and they asked him his name and where he went to school. Ryan told John to come and sit with him and Sam.

John was beginning to feel welcome here.

John noticed another poster on another wall, which read: **Love your neighbor as yourself. Matthew 19:19**

When everyone sat back down, _____ _____
began to cry. John had heard the leader say their new
daughter (being held in the back by her mom) had been
sick and asked that the kids stop and pray for her. Wow,
John thought as he listened to the kids pray. Several
kids prayed aloud and sounded like they knew God
personally and actually believed he would do what they
asked. John had never prayed before, because he never
knew the right words to say. These kids just talked to
God like a real person!

Just as the lesson began, a mouse began to _____
across the room, and Beth saw it first. She shrieked and
jumped up on a chair. The whole group screamed as the
mouse ran under a desk. The leader stopped the lesson,
and then the hunt began. One kid got a broom, another got
a box, and everyone scrambled to catch this pest. John was
amused by the whole situation, as his dad owned a pest
control company, and he wasn't afraid of the little mouse.
He offered to dispose of the mouse when the leader finally
caught it. The other kids thought he was a hero.

After everyone settled back down, the leader began to
talk. He talked about the things we do and the choices we
make, and how one day there will be a _____ _____,
when we will receive a reward for the life we've lived. If
we have lived a life of sin, we will receive eternal death.
However, if we have believed in Jesus and asked him to
forgive us our sins, we will be rewarded with an eternal
life full of joy, peace and fellowship with God and other
believers. John wanted this kind of life. He had seen what
sin can do to a person, as his uncle had recently died
because he drank too much and had a car accident. His
grandmother was mean and bitter and hated everyone
who tried to talk to her.

John didn't want to be sad and lonely, and he wanted to help his grandmother feel better.

The leaders read: *Romans 6:23: The wages of sin is death, but the gift of God is eternal life in Christ Jesus our Lord.*

Mr. _____ and his son _____ (John found their names amusing) came over to pray with John when he raised his hand to receive Christ into his heart. What kind people are here tonight, he thought. He had seen them have fun, worship together, be kind to him and listen intently to life-changing lessons from their leader. He wanted to be a part of such a group, and he wanted to be free from sin and receive the gift of eternal life.

After the service was over, John and the kids went outside to play basketball. John didn't feel like the "new" person anymore. What fun he had. He came back week after week and brought other friends with him. These kids lived what they believed. They had been kind to him, though he was a stranger. They had worshiped their God unashamed. They had shared the gift of life with him, by their enjoyment of God and by letting it show.

Isn't life supposed to be like the above story? Good friends worshipping together, laughing together and inviting others to join in with them? Be sure that you notice newcomers to your group or family and make them feel welcome. Enjoy your life and let it show. You never know when the smile you're wearing, the fun you're having and the joy you're showing just might be contagious to someone else who is watching.

Enjoy your life, enjoy God and enjoy the new people he brings into your path…

FRUITS OF THE SPIRIT

The purpose of this study is to taste and see the fruits of the spirit, and learn how they are to be alive in our hearts.

Preparation: Cut up the following fruits and place one or more of each kind in parfait cups or bowls, one bowl for each person. Provide toothpicks.

How to implement this study: *Follow the study below, reading the definition of each fruit of the spirit, and then eat the fruit in the bowl that corresponds.* Talk about how the spiritual fruit is similar to the fruit they are eating, as written in the parentheses by each one. Discuss each fruit and how it can grow in our lives.

Read ***Galatians 5:22, 23*** aloud. Talk about how fruit grows on a tree, it has to be watered, receive sunlight, etc. and how a tree is known/called by the fruit it bears.

LOVE (strawberries, red, heart-shaped, sweet and can be extra sweet when chocolate-covered) – profound tender or passionate affection for a person.

JOY (grapes – round and fun, easy to eat, tasty) – great delight or happiness caused by something good or satisfying.

PEACE (pears – mild flavor, soothing) – freedom of the mind from annoyance, distraction, anxiety, etc.

PATIENCE (kiwi – takes time to peel, not very common) – bearing annoyance, affliction or pain without complaint, loss of temper, irritation or the like.

KINDNESS (orange – full of vitamin c, good for the health of the body) – quality of having a giving, considerate and helpful nature.

GOODNESS (mandarin orange – usually sold when processed and put into cans – we are only good when we are in Jesus, his righteousness, not ours) – moral excellence or virtue, uprightness, only achieved through knowing Jesus.

FAITHFULNESS (lemon – sharp taste, and when salt is added, has an even stronger bite, like faith with works) – steady in allegiance to God's word and promises, fully believing them.

GENTLENESS (banana – soft fruit, soft answers) – quality of being mild; not severe, rough or violent.

SELF-CONTROL (apple – what symbolized Eve's lack of self-control, can for us be a reminder of how with God we can have self-control) – restraint of one's actions or feelings.

Fruit is produced after the plant has been planted, watered and taken well care of. *Pray together for these fruits to be evident in your life.*

He is God

This study instructs us on the fact that He is God and we are not.

Preparation: Gather lint from your dryer screen for a couple of weeks until you have about a cup or more of lint for each person participating. On the table, have a cup of water and a small pack of garden seeds. Give each one a piece of foil or a paper plate for their work space. Have a trash can available for all to use.

How to implement this study: Sit around a table so each one has a work space. Give each one their cup of lint and have them divide it into six equal pieces.

He is God. We are man. However, sometimes we think we know better than God and we wonder why he does what he does. Sometimes things happen in our lives that make us wonder about God, who he is, if he really is in control of our lives, if he really is so powerful, if he really is aware of us, etc.

The book of Job is about a man who lost everything. In chapter 31 he begins to question what has happened to him and why. Sometimes when we have an unanswered prayer, we question why. When there is great sorrow around us, we question why. After Job began questioning God, God sent a long answer in chapters 38-41. He wanted to make sure Job knew that he was God.

****

Read Genesis 2:7: God formed man from the dust of the earth.
Take your dust and form a person. Now blow on it. What happened? Were you able to form a person? **He is God.**

We are man. You are alive because God breathed life into your soul. You will stay alive by his might and power. You are in his hands. When we see dust, we want to wipe it away, it's bothersome. When God saw dust, he formed man in his own image, it was lovely. *Toss your unformed, dead as can be lint, into the trash.*

****

Read Gen. 1:1, 9: God created the heavens and the earth, and the waters and the dry land.

Form a ball from your dust, resembling the earth. Now sprinkle water over the earth that you've made. Does it look good? It looks like a blob of dust that got wet, right? **He is God. We are man.** He's got the whole world in his hand and he is in control of everything that goes on down here. After all, he created it! *Toss your soggy dust ball into the trash.*

****

Job 38 is God's response back to Job, after he begins to wonder and question God.

Read Job 38: 25-27, 37-38. God is in control of the skies.

Make cloud formations out of your dust. Now speak to them and make them rain. Can you do it? **He is God. We are man.** He sends the rain, he makes the sun shine and he places the stars in correct alignment. All of creation testifies of God's awesome power and might. No need to worry, he knows when it's raining in your life. He can speak one word and calm the storm. *Blow your clouds into the trash.*

****

Read Isaiah 1:18. Sin makes our hearts dark. Jesus alone brings light and forgiveness.

Form a heart with your lint. Now rid the heart of all dirt and dust. You would have to throw away the whole heart, because it is made from dirt and dust. We are born into this world with a heart full of sin. We need a savior and God sent his son to be the perfect sacrifice. **He is God. We are man.** He can take a heart that is full of sin, and make it clean again. *Get rid of your filthy, dusty hearts.*

****

Read Isaiah 55: 8-11. God makes things grow and accomplishes what he will,with just a word.

Spread out your lint out to make a garden. Sprinkle some seeds into your "dirt". Now make the sun shine, send rain and make the seeds grow. We can't do it. We can plant seeds in a garden, but we depend on the rain and the sun to make them grow. God created something so intricate and amazing inside of every seed that makes that tiny speck grow into a huge plant. We can't even comprehend such amazing creativity and power. **He is God. We are man.** *Sweep away your pitiful "garden" into the trash.*

****

Read Isaiah 64:8. He is our Father. He is the potter. We are the clay.

Try to make a pot out of a little water and your dirt. Is it hard to form it? Will it hold water? God's hands form us and make us into a beautiful vessel of honor for him. **He is God. We are man.** The clay does not talk to the potter and tell him what to do, or how to be shaped and formed. The potter has a creation in mind, a purpose for the clay, before he ever begins. *Squish your "pot" into a tiny ball and toss it away.*

****

Read Job 42:1-6 to read of Job's reply back to God, after God reminded him of his power and his rule over all the earth.

God can do all things (after all, look at all of creation).
No plan of his can be thwarted (he is in control)
We cannot understand God's ways (his ways are higher than ours)
God speaks and we should listen (he loves us so much)
We need to repent of doubt and unbelief (he is worthy of our complete trust).

Even our best attempts at trying to control the world around us, create new things out of the old, making ourselves pure, calming the storms in our lives, etc. are all futile. **He is God. We are man.** It's okay to wonder sometimes about the world and why God does what he does, but instead of wondering, get out your Bible and read the chapters mentioned at the beginning of the study, and remind yourself of the awesomeness of God. You really can face whatever comes your way, because he knows, he cares, and he's the one in control. You really can trust in Him.

Sing together "He's got the Whole World in his Hands", and then pray and ask God to forgive you for the times you doubt his love and care.

HOUSE OF BRICK

This study uses the story of the three little pigs to demonstrate the importance of a strong house.

Preparation: You will need three "smokies" (small sausages) for the three pigs, and someone to act as the wolf, (someone who can blow very hard!) You will need a can of shoestring potatoes, a small bag of stick pretzels, a large chocolate bar (that can be separated into rectangles) and one piece of candy corn.

How to implement this study: The story of the three little pigs will be acted out with the props mentioned above, to demonstrate the importance of building a strong, firm "house" that will stand against all of the attacks against it.

The Bible speaks clearly about the importance of building a strong house with a good foundation, one that has Jesus as the chief cornerstone and one that houses the Holy Spirit. The three little pigs in the following story are building houses to protect themselves from the "big, bad wolf", so let's see what happened and what we can learn from their story.

The first little pig built his house out of straw because that was the easiest way to go. However, a house made of straw is not very strong when winds begin to blow, and it is certainly not fireproof. A straw house is easily broken into. *(pile up a handful of shoestring potatoes to represent the straw house).*

The second little pig was a little more ambitious and he built his house out of sticks. Now sticks are a bit sturdier than straw, will hold up a little longer than straw, but are certainly not fireproof either. This house is easily destroyed through the slightest of storms. *(Lay the pretzels across each other to build a house of sticks).*

The third pig was the wisest pig and he knew about building strong houses, so he chose brick for his house. Bricks could stand firm against wind, and were the best choice for a strong, sturdy and safe house. *(Stack the chocolate "bricks" around in a rectangle, leaving a space in the middle). (Place one "pig" at each house).*

There was a Wolf who lived near these houses and he would tease and taunt the three pigs, "Let me in! Let me in! I'll huff and I"ll puff and I'll blow your house in." he would cry. Each pig would reply back, "Not by the hair of my chinny, chin, chin!" *(Have the wolf ready to "blow" as you continue to read...)*

The wolf came to the first house made of straw, made his threats and blew the house down, sending the first little pig running...*(have the wolf blow and knock over the house of straw, but have the pig flee with a couple of the potatoes in his hand)*

55

The wolf came to the second house made of sticks, made his threats and blew the house down, and sent the second pig running…(*knock over the house of sticks, but have the pig flee with a couples of sticks in his hand*)

The two pigs then fled to the third pig's house, carrying pieces of their houses, to remind them of their loss. The third pig was safe in his well-built house and welcomed the two other pigs. When the wolf arrived, they were ready and waiting with a huge fire in the fireplace. (*place the potatoes and sticks in the middle of the brick house, with a candy corn in the middle, representing the fire*) When the wolf threatened and saw that he could not blow the house down, he tried to sneak in through the chimney. He met his death when he fell into the fire. (*The wolf's mouth is closed and can blow no more*).

The pigs danced and rejoiced in their safe house after the wolf was gone, because he could no longer bother them anymore…

What can we learn from this story?

1. The first pig was hasty, lazy and foolish. Hay is just dried up grass and very flammable. When we try to breeze our way through life, being lazy in our love for God and foolish in our actions, our house just might not stand too well when a big wind blows.

2. The second pig was a little more thoughtful, but still used sticks that were lying around because they were easy to gather. He still was unwise, as he built a house that was easily disturbed.

3. The third pig was thoughtful, diligent and wise. He knew his house needed to be strong, so he took care and

time to build it firmly. He knew his house needed to be a safe place for others, so made sure it would stand. He knew there was a big wind coming and he made his house out of solid brick.

4. Finally, we notice that the two other pigs used their leftover pieces of their house to build the fire in the third pig's house. Even though their houses had fallen in the big puffs from the wolf, God used their failures to build a fire that destroyed that same wolf. Even when we fail at things we do, God will use these failures to make us strong. The brick house was strong and had the fire of life inside, so even when it seemed as if the wolf had found a way in, he met his death when he encountered the fire.

Read Ephesians 2:19-22; Psalm 127:1; I Corinthians 3:10-15.

Are you full of fire?
Is your house strong?

Jesus must be the center of everything you do, your foundation must be the word of God and you need to be filled with the spirit of God. These are the materials for a "house of brick". Then you too can dance around and sing, "Who's afraid of the big bad wolf, the big bad wolf...???" "Not me!"

(Pour the straw, sticks and bricks in a bowl, mix and enjoy a fun snack together).

HOW TO DEAL

This lesson teaches us "how to deal" with things that we experience in life.

Preparation: A regular card deck is needed.

How to implement this study: Read over the card activities in parentheses below, then go through each "life experience", demonstrating each real life "deal" with a deal of the cards. (*You may want to practice the card trick before using it in the study.*)

Accidents (*spill the cards on the floor*) – talk about how we all have "spills" from time to time, and we should all be willing to help out each other.(*have everyone help pick up cards one by one) I Cor. 12:25, 26* .

Losses (*deal out five cards to each person, add the values and see who has the losing hand*). Talk about losing a game or losing a friend who moves, etc. (Find something to be thankful about in times of loss and be patient, another "hand" is coming your way…) *II Cor. 4:16,17*

Embarrassment *(Deal out cards, with one person receiving the joker)* – talk about being embarrassed and how it feels, how to deal with it. (*Ask the person with the joker to reveal it and laugh along)* – make sure we don't cause the embarrassment to someone else and when we are embarrassed, learn to laugh at ourselves. *Prov. 17:22.*

Victory (Deal out five cards again, see who has the winning hand) – be humble, don't gloat. If someone else wins, be happy, not jealous. *Rom 12:15, 16.*

Not understanding – *(do a card trick, (one is provided below),* showing how we don't understand how it is done, because we don't understand the process) we might think life's "not fair" or we don't understand why we get in trouble and someone else doesn't – we must realize we don't understand everything, but we have to trust. We have to trust our parents, and God. ***Prov. 3:5,6***

Feeling left out (deal out cards, forgetting one person altogether) – talk about how that feels, and how to deal. We need to make sure we include everyone when we're with friends, and if we're the one being left out, don't take it personally. It's okay to feel hurt, but forgive and go on. ***Matt. 6:12.*** Forgive those who leave you out and ask forgiveness when you leave out someone else.

Finally, *(lay out the King of Hearts in the center of the table)* –

Psalm 47:7 God is our King and he is the one who can make everything work together for our good. So no matter what you are "dealt" in life, the King of Hearts (Jesus) is in control.

FOUR FRIENDLY KINGS

Do the first 3 steps away from your audience or pre-prepared.

1) Take the four Kings out of the deck, and also two other cards.

2) Fan the four Kings out, and place the two other cards you selected behind the second King. Line them up so your audience cannot see the two other cards.

3) Show the Kings to the spectators.

4) Place the Kings (and the two secret cards) face down on the top of the deck.

5) Tell the audience that the four Kings are good friends, and they don't let anything get between them.

6) Place the top King on the bottom of the deck. You may show the audience this card.

7) Place the next card (not a King) into the center of the deck.

8) Repeat step 7.

9) Leave the fourth card on the top. You may show the audience that it is a King.

10) Explain that the Kings are real good friends and will soon be back together.

11) Cut the deck in the middle, and put the bottom half on the top.

12) Search the deck for the four Kings. They have been magically moved next to each other.

Trick courtesy of: nick@empire.net

I See

This study helps us to open our eyes and see the needs of others around us.

Preparation: Assign the following characters: old man, young girl, young boy, teenager (with a skateboard or skates) and narrator. Set up a bench (piano bench, or chair). The old man should wear a coat and have a cane (large umbrella will do). To the side of the bench, set a pitcher of cool water and a cup on a small table. Place some fresh cut flowers on the table (options: use artificial flowers or a flower garden if one is available nearby).

How to implement this study: If it's a nice day, have this study outside. Give each character a copy of the study and assign their lines: The old man's lines are in **bold**, the young girl's lines are underlined, the young boy's are in CAPITALS and the **teenager's** lines are in ***bold italics.***

Narrator begins to read: Sometimes people who once had perfectly good eyes cannot see anymore. People who could hear pretty songs no longer hear any music at all. And there are many who once had a skip in their step but now can barely even walk. What a sad way to go through life, not enjoying the things around you, not hearing beautiful melodies and dragging your feet when trying to move. Let's observe a pretty day in a park and "see" what happens:

An old man was sitting on a park bench. He was mostly blind, partially deaf and walked with a cane. He came to the park every day to sit and wait. He didn't know what he was waiting for, but he waited. He was wrapped in a heavy coat and very sad. He had no friends and no one really wanted to be his friend.

A young girl was walking through the park with her dog. "Look at the beautiful flowers!" she exclaimed out loud. She walked behind the bench where the old man was seated and took in a deep breath. "They smell wonderful!" she said out loud, again. The old man coughed and grunted, **"The flowers will just die when the sun gets hot."** The young girl replied, "Oh yes, but can't you see their beauty now? And after they die, next spring they'll be here again. I love to look at them." *(Young girl holds the flowers and smiles. She then sits on the ground near the bench.)*

The very next minute, there was a table being set up near the bench where the old man was seated. (*Young boy is seated at the table, pretending to set things up.*) The old man could barely hear the chatter of those near by. "I hope we collect lots of money for the poor," stated one lady. "Do you think anyone will buy our crafts?" asked a young child. "This is so exciting" stated a girl. The old man grunted and said out loud, **"There's nothing but rich people around here. Snobby, no good, selfish rich people. You won't do any good here!"** The young boy from the table came over to the man and explained that the youth group at his church was selling crafts they'd made, to give to the poor in Africa.

"CAN'T YOU SEE, MISTER, THERE ARE POOR PEOPLE ALL OVER THE WORLD WHO NEED OUR HELP. WOULD YOU LIKE TO BUY SOMETHING?!" stated the young boy. The old man turned his face away. (*Young boy walks back to the table*). The man was getting frustrated with all the commotion around him and he tried to get up to move to another bench. As he stood up, he dropped his cane.

A teenager was skating by and stopped to pick up the cane and hand it to the old man. *"I see that you dropped your cane. Here you go,"* said the teenager as he gently placed the cane in the old man's hand. **"Go away. I can get around by myself"** retorted the old man. The teenager just smiled and gave the old man a gentle pat on the hand as he walked on.

The old man decided it was too far to walk to the next bench so he just moved a few steps and sat on the other end of the bench. Why couldn't everyone just let him be? Girls looking at pretty flowers, people giving to the poor, and some young kid offering him help, it was all too much. His bench used to be his place, his quiet place, to sit and wait. Now everyone was bothering him.

About that time, the young girl with flowers came back by and had a bunch of flowers in her hand. "Here", she said, as she placed the bouquet in his gnarled fingers. She had to pry his hands open to place them there. "I see that you are all alone and I thought that if you smelled this wonderful bunch of flowers, it might brighten your day." The old man loosened his grip a little and let her place the flowers in his hands. The young girl even had the nerve to sit down beside him on the bench and start swinging her feet! Why was she so happy?

The young boy from the craft table came over and started talking to the young girl. He was getting hot standing in the direct sun and he noticed the old many was wiping his forehead.

The boy went to the table and got a cold cup of water and came back to the bench. "HERE, I SEE THAT YOU ARE HOT LIKE I AM. HAVE A DRINK OF COOL WATER", the boy told the old man. **"Are you talking to me?"** replied the old man. "YES, WE HAVE LOTS OF COLD

WATER AT OUR TABLE OVER THERE AND I WANT YOU TO HAVE A CUP. DRINK ALL YOU WANT. THERE IS LOTS MORE WATER WHERE THIS CAME FROM." The old man laid the flowers on his lap and reached for the water. My, it tasted good. No one had ever offered him a drink, in all the years he had been sitting on this same bench.

The man sat on the bench and smelled the flowers. He felt satisfied from the cool drink of water the young boy has shared with him. He even began to listen to the tune the young girl was humming beside him. She started singing a few words, "Jesus loves me, this I know…" Wait, he recognized those words. He had heard them when he was a little boy, when he went to church one time. Lots of years had gone by since that time. He had grown up, fought in a war, married his lovely wife who was now gone, never had any children, lost his home in a fire and then he had grown old so fast.

Just then, the teenager on the skateboard rode up again. The young girl left the bench and skipped away, as the teenager sat down, out of breath. *"It's hot,"* he said. **"Yeah"**, said the old man. The teenager kept sitting on the bench. The old man's eyes were not good, but he could make out a sad expression on the boy's face and thought he might have seen a tear. He remembered that the teenager had tried to hand him his cane when he dropped it, and the old man remembered that he had been rude to the boy.

"Just wanted to say thanks for handing me my cane" the old man said gruffly, yet softly. *"You're welcome,"* said the teen, as he sniffled a little. **"I see you're sad,"** the old man turned and said. **"Here, smell these flowers. They're really nice."** The old man got up, forgetting the pain in his knees, and shuffled over to the table to ask for another cup of water. He shuffled back and handed the boy the cup of cold water. **"Here, drink up."**

"Why are you being so nice to me?" asked the teenager. **"I saw that you looked sad,"** said the old man. *"Can I sit by you a while?"* asked the teen. *"I just moved here and I don't have any friends."* The old man smiled and sat back down. Somehow his eyesight was a little clearer, his hearing was a little keener and his steps were a little surer.

The old man and the teen sat for hours on the bench. (*Old man puts his arm around the teenager*). The old man told the young teen stories of his childhood, and the teenager listened and laughed. The good people at the table sold lots of crafts and made lots of money for the poor. The flowers stood tall as they reached toward the sun, and the breeze of the late afternoon sent their sweet aroma to all who walked by. A young girl was skipping through the park, and a young man and an old man sat together smiling, as the sun slid down the sky in colors of gold and purple, preparing to sleep for the night.

The old man was a grumbler. That means he complained a lot. Obviously, when we get old physically, our eyesight grows dim, our hearing may wane and our legs might not work like they used to. However, the bible says even though our outward man perishes, our inward man is renewed day by day. This old man is an example in his physical body of the way we can become in our spiritual walk, if we're not careful. Grumbling leads to discontentment and discontentment leads to growing old and dry, spiritually. Remember the story of Moses leading the Children of Israel out of Eqypt into the wilderness? God delivered them from bondage and set them free...*Read Exodus 15: 24*. When the Children of

Israel were in the wilderness they grew thirsty and grumbled. They had already forgotten that God had promised if they obeyed him, he would bless them. And so they grumbled. The old man had forgotten the good things in his life, so he grumbled, even when he was offered a cool drink of water. *Read Exodus 16:2,3.* Again these people are grumbling. This time they were hungry. Again they didn't think to trust God and see that he was with them. The old man couldn't see or smell the beautiful flowers because he was focused on the missing things in his life. *Read Exodus 32:1.* These people never learned. They continued to grumble, and this time it was because they were impatient. Impatience caused them to sin by making idols to worship instead of the true, living God. The old man in the story had grown impatient with those around him and didn't want to be bothered. His impatience caused him to act mean and say mean things.

Thankfully, the story we read ended well. The old man realized the beauty around him and allowed himself to be happy. After he received a cup of cold water, he offered a cup of cold water to someone else. And finally, he gave of himself to listen and be a friend to someone else in need. Even though his physical body was old, his spiritual man was awakened by the deeds of others around him and he was able to look and see that he still had a wonderful life to live and blessings to share…

Grumbling…discontment…impatience…despair…I don't want to go there.
Seeing….hearing…smelling…touching….I do want to care.
I am blessed by the kindness of others. I am blessed by the goodness of God.
I am followed by goodness and mercy wherever I go….this I know…
Because Jesus loves me so.

Irritations

This study brings attention to the irritations in life and how to get rid of them.

Preparation: Have each person prepare themselves by adding the following irritations, one to a person, or one person can have more than one: a belt that is too tight, an ankle brace, hair combed down over the face (give this person a comb), a watch around an ankle, weights, toilet paper hanging off their shoe, a rock in their shoe and something sticky (like honey) on their hand (give this person a wet cloth). Each irritation is not to be spoken about or demonstrated until you get to each one as you study. The point is for each person to actually feel "irritated" throughout the study, until they are asked to lay down (get rid of) their irritation.

How to implement this study: As you follow along below, let the person with that irritation stand up and note what is irritating them, and say "I'm so irritated!" There are common everyday irritations that can be paralleled to common spiritual irritations. Each irritation listed below has the solution at the end of the phrase.

"My belt is too tight." ....well....**loosen it!** Sometimes we're too hard on ourselves and make ourselves uncomfortable just because we aren't able to relax. Making good grades and doing well at sports are examples of where we sometimes put too much pressure on ourselves to be perfect. Loosen up, do your best, and enjoy your life…you can experience freedom in Christ. *(Read II Cor. 3:17)*.

"I have an old injury and I'm afraid to walk again.".. well...get free from the fear! Sometimes our fears and hurts we have almost cripple us. But the truth is that Jesus is with us and he gives us strength, so we don't have to be afraid. He says you are his child, so take off the brace (the fear) and run with him, free of fear! *(Read Psalm 46:1,2).*

"I can't see why everyone around me is so irritating"... well...move away what's covering your eyes! Sometimes all we see in others is their faults, when we have big faults of our own, like hair hanging down in our eyes! We need to first clear up our own vision, so we can see clearly the beauty in others around us. *(Read Matthew 7:1-3)*

"Something just always feels out of place, I just don't fit in"...well...find the place where you're supposed to be and be content! Sometimes we feel like an outsider, at school or church, never quite fitting in with others. The truth is that you do fit into the kingdom of God, you have a special place in God's heart, and you can find your place and feel comfortable in being who God made you to be. *(Read Prov. 19:23).*

"I'm always weighed down, like I can barely move." ... well...lay down your burdens at Jesus' feet. Sometimes we carry around "extra weight" that Jesus never intended for us to carry. All the things we've mentioned so far, like fear, competition, hurt, etc. are weights we don't have to have hanging around on us. Lay them down and see how much better you will feel! *(Read Psalm 68:19).*

"I feel like people are always laughing at me."... Well...trade the embarrassment for God's approval of the way he made you. Sometimes we feel embarrassed by our looks or ways that make us different than others around us. *(Read Psalm 139:14)* and be thankful that you are made the way you are, with the looks and talents you have.

"Something is always rubbing me the wrong way." … well…get rid of the source of irritation! Sometimes we carry around a grudge against someone and it's like having a rock in our shoe, it bothers us with every step we take. The only way to get rid of this irritation is to take out the rock and throw it away! *(Read I Cor. 13:4,5).*

"I never feel really clean."…well…come to Jesus and his blood can wash you whiter than snow. Sometimes there is sin, or just old feelings or habits that stick to us and we just can't seem to shake them off. Jesus is the one who can take away every irritation, sin, bad habit, bad thought, etc. and give us clean hands and pure hearts, free from irritation. *(Read Psalm 24:3,4).*

Jesus is the only one who can truly relieve our tired, irritated souls...

One by one, have each person lay their source of irritation down, as if they're laying it at the feet of Jesus. Have them state what it is that they are laying down. For example, "I'm laying down my belt, because I'm going to loosen up and relax, and not be so hard on myself", etc.

Pray together that these irritations will remain where they were placed, at the feet of Jesus.

IT'S WHAT's INSIDE
THAT COUNTS

This study shows us that the inside of our heart is what is important.

Preparation: You will need a Poptart (or other fruit-filled pastry), a book that has had the cover changed, an empty wallet (with a dollar to insert later), a pen that is dried up or is empty, a flashlight with no batteries (with the batteries available), a dirty cup (with a towel to clean it) and a Bible.

How to implement this study: This study teaches that the inside is what's important to God, so that is what should be important to us. Just follow along below:

Man looks on the outward appearance, but God looks at the heart. (I Sam 16:7b)

Some things are hard and crusty on the outside, but soft and tasty on the inside (*take a bite of the pastry*) **– Sometimes we are like this, too. We sometimes make it hard for people to get to know us, but if they do, they find out we're pretty sweet. Be sure that if you take the time to make your outside look nice, the inside is just as nice, as well.** *(Read Gal. 5:22).*

A book is often chosen because of the picture or title on the cover. (*Open the book and notice the title does not match the content*). But what if the covers get switched? And what if the inside of the book is not what is advertised on the cover? Sometimes we advertise ourselves to be Christians, but when people get to see the real us, they see something totally different. Let's make sure what our "cover" says actually describes who we are, a follower of Jesus Christ, who loves others with all our hearts. In other words, don't be ashamed of who you are and what you stand for. (*Read Rom. 1:16*). *(take the wrong cover off and replace it with the one that matches)*

A pen can be a useful tool, if it actually writes! But if the inside is dry, the pen needs to be thrown away or refilled! We can be useful for God's kingdom if we're full and have something to give, but if we're dry and thirsty, we're not much use to anyone. *(Read II Tim. 2:21). (either throw away the pen, or put the ink back in it, and show that it works now)*

A **flashlight** **is a necessity in the dark, and can be the difference between stumbling and walking on a clear path. But if the batteries are missing inside, which is the source of energy to make the battery work, the flashlight won't help at all! Trying to walk in the light, when you are really in the dark, will cause you to stumble and bring others tumbling down with you.** *(Read I John 1: 5-7). (Insert the batteries and shine the light!)*

When you are asked to give, it's nice to have money in your wallet to share. But if your wallet is always empty, something's wrong. You need to make deposits into your wallet, so you'll be ready to give when you see an opportunity. You also need to make "deposits" into your spirit, by being faithful to worship with other Christians, so you will have spiritual blessings to pour out on others. *(Read II Corinthians. 9:6-8). (Insert a dollar into the wallet, demonstrating keeping it filled)*

Would you like to drink out of a cup that is dirty or eat with a spoon that's been used? No way. You want your food to be served in clean dishes. If we offer a "drink" to someone, they will back off if they see the cup we're offering is dirty inside. Keep yourself clean, so that when you offer someone a drink, it will be received gladly. *(Read Matt. 23:25, 26) (wipe the dish clean).*

What good is your Bible if it is never opened and read on the inside? It's what's on the inside that counts! Carrying your Bible with you to church is good, but opening it and reading it daily is what counts, so that the word of God lives inside of us. *(Read Col. 3:16). (state that during this study, you have been depositing the word into your mind and heart).*

Finally, remember the story of Noah's ark? Those who were on the inside were the ones who were safe from the floods. Those left on the outside were destroyed by the flood. The only place of safety was inside the boat that God had Noah build for his family and the animals. *(Read Gen. 7:1, 5, 8: 15-19) (Because Noah obeyed and went inside as God commanded, he not only was safe, but blessed).*

Read the following paragraph together, and have the family say aloud the capitalized words. Then pray together.

Living together as a family INSIDE a house and home is very important, as it was to Noah and his family, to be INSIDE the ark. There is safety and blessing INSIDE a home full of people who obey and love God. However, when it is time to come OUTSIDE the home, we are to be fruitful for God and multiply his kingdom. Because we were safe and blessed INSIDE the home, when we go OUTSIDE, that protection goes with us wherever we go. What goes on INSIDE the home affects what happens OUTSIDE the home.
It's what on the INSIDE that counts!

JOURNALING

This study demonstrates the need for writing things down.

Preparation: You will need a journal for each person participating. You can make a journal with blank paper tied together with yarn, or purchase a blank book or spiral for each person. Along with each journal, hand each person the following: a post-it, a piece of paper from a long notepad, a week calendar, a piece of scratch paper (crinkly torn piece), lined paper, one piece of construction paper and a piece of blank drawing paper (The calendar, lined paper and blank paper are provided on the last page. Make a copy and cut out for each person). Provide scissors, markers or crayons, pencils or pens, and glue or tape.

How to implement this study: Hand each person their own personal "journal", along with their pieces of paper, and get started. As each paragraph below is read, do what is instructed in italics and glue or tape each piece of paper into your personal journals.

Read Psalm 79:13 *Keeping a personal journal that reflects our life is a good thing to do. We are going to create a journal that can be used whenever we have time to sit and meditate on God and his goodness to us, whenever we have time to reflect on our day's activities, whenever we have time to be creative, etc. It is good to "recount his praise". In other words, it is good to sit down, meditate on God's goodness in our lives and then write our thoughts and expressions down on paper.*

Post-it – These little squares are often used for reminders, because you can stick them anywhere. We might need to remember a gift we need to take to someone, so we post a sticky note on the door reminding us to take it when we leave. Let's write on our post-it a note to ourselves to remember to write in our journals. (*Write on the note "Remember to write" and stick the note on the front of your journal*).

A long skinny notepad is usually used to make a **list**. When we go to the store, we need a list of things to buy. When we have many chores to do, maybe our parents hands us a list of things to do. A list is handy so you don't have to store so much information in your memory. You can just pull out the list and look at it. It's fun to check off the things on the list as they are completed. Let's make a list of cool scriptures, five of them, and then check them off next week as you read them, and then you can make another. Keep a running list of your favorite scriptures..(*Write these scripture verses on the list: Psalm 100: 1,2; Proverbs 3:3; Matthew 22:37; Romans 6:23; Ephesians 5:1,2. Glue or tape the list on the first page of the journal.*)

Calendar – A calendar lets you plan ahead. You can plan sleepovers with friends, write down parties you've been invited to, your friends' birthdays, etc. It's important to plan and schedule events, so you can look forward to them and make room in your schedule for them. We're going to insert a calendar with days of the week, and glue it in our journals. (*Glue in calendar*). Think of any activities you have planned for the next week and fill them in. *Now write the following on any three days you choose: "do something kind, pray for a friend, thank someone today".* Remember to read your calendar and do these things!

Scratch paper - This piece of paper is usually wrinkled and old, and we use it when we can't find anything else to write on. We might just decide to "doodle" on the paper just for fun. *(Try doodling anything that you feel like doodling on the paper and glue it into your journal.)* Take time to doodle sometimes, it feels good. It's always good to relax. Look at the doodling of each other and observe the differences. Some people doodle flowers, others doodle geometric shapes and some people write curvy lines.

Notebook paper - A fresh clean piece of paper with lines is so inviting. There are plenty of lines for writing a full paragraph. When we have time, we should write down a story, something about our day, a letter to a friend, or whatever comes to mind. This page is for thinking before we write. We could even just write a letter to God, telling him how we feel or a letter of thanksgiving and praise. (*Write two sentences of thanksgiving about your day on the lined paper and glue it in your journal*).

Construction paper is just that – paper used for constructing something. Construction paper comes in many colors and it's easy to cut and bend. Try your hand at creativity with your piece of construction paper. Cut it into shapes and then glue them into your journal in a creative pattern. See what you come up with! (*Cut up the construction paper, create and glue*).

Blank white paper - Wow. We can draw, sketch or color a beautiful picture of anything we want. Look around the room and sketch something you see, or think of a picture and sketch what you see in your mind. You might want to close your eyes and let your hand just draw. *(After you have sketched, glue the drawing in your journal.)*

Now that you have entered a list, a calendar, a doodle, an art piece and a drawing, you have several creative ideas for your journal. Keep the journal near your bed and when you have the time, rest and reflect on God's goodness, on his mercy, on his Word, on his blessings, and let your creativity flow by adding more entries until you have a full book! Remember to read your verses and look at your calendar next week.

Calendar for the week

Sunday	Monday	Tuesday	Wednesday	Thursday	Friday	

Lined paper

Paper for drawing

Just a little won't hurt... will it?

This study is about how sin is bad, period.

Preparation: You will need to have a door mostly closed, but open just a little, in view while you study. You also need a match, a piece of paper, some cayenne pepper (or other hot spice), a permanent marker, a plastic or Styrofoam cup with a small hole or crack in it, some hand weights, and a magazine with a page half torn loose.

How to implement this study: This study demonstrates how even the sins we think are "small" and "won't hurt" to try, are still sin and can have negative, long-lasting effects on our lives and others around us. Just read over the lesson and have things set up, where you can demonstrate each concept. **Make sure you, the adult, demonstrate the fire concept.**

Read **Psalm 119:133**, making this verse the central theme of your lesson.

Have you ever been tempted to do something wrong, to just try a little sin? After all, what would it hurt? Just a little lie, just a little wrong, just to see what it feels like to do something you know is not right? Let's look at some ways that even a little wrong can cause a lot of pain...

(Point to the door that is open just a crack, and talk about how tempting it is to look inside, especially if we know we're not supposed to). **Sometimes we are tempted to just take a peek at something we know wouldn't be right. Reading or viewing things that are not pleasing to God could make us feel things and thinks things that could harm us. (*Read Prov. 17:24*).**

There's no such thing as a little fire. (*light the paper and show how quickly it spreads, and then blow out the fire*). Gossip and lying is just like fire. Once it gets started, it spreads and grows, hurting everyone it touches. *(Read James 3:5,6).*

A cook knows that it only takes a little dash of a strong spice to flavor a whole pot. (*Place a dash of pepper on your finger and taste it*). Even just a little taste of sin can affect our whole heart and a lot of other people. There is no "little" sin, as all sin is not pleasing to God and leaves a bad taste in our mouth and His. Let's make sure what we "taste" is the goodness of God, so there is no room for even a taste of sin. (*Read Psalm 119:103,104).*

When we just get a little mark of permanent ink on our clothes, it spreads and permanently ruins the clothing. (*hold a permanent marker in one spot on a piece of paper or a scrap of cloth, and show how the ink spread)* **Even just a little lie can permanently ruin a friendship or trust between two people. (*Read Prov. 26:28*).**

Just a small crack in a cup or glass, which is sometimes not even visible, allows the liquid inside to leak out and eventually the cup is empty. (*pour a bit of water in the cracked cup and watch it seep through*). Just a small sin can be like a small crack, hardly noticeable at first. But if the crack is not fixed properly, it will grow and grow until we are hardly useful as a Christian. But Jesus is faithful to forgive our sins and repair our "cracks", if we just ask. (*Read I John 1:9).*

The weight of sin is too heavy to bear. (*Pick up the weight and imagine carrying a heavy weight around all day*). It makes us feel very uncomfortable. Little sins may feel like nothing at first, but as you sin over and over again, the weight is too heavy, because you are not supposed to carry around sin in your heart. *(Read Heb. 12:1-3).*

A page in a book begins to tear just a bit at the edge. (*Find the loose page*) Then with continued use, the page eventually

just rips loose from the binding. Sin is like that. We just try to get by with doing something we think is just a little wrong, and eventually we fall away from the place we belong, bound to the word of God within us. (*Read Prov. 3:3,4*).

Don't try to get by with a "little" sin in your life. "Just a little" may eventually be "just too much." Always confess your sins and let Jesus make you strong to stand against every temptation to sin.

KEEPING FIT

This study will work out our bodies, as well as our spirits.

Preparation: Find a large area where the family can sit down in a circle and have room to exercise. Have a CD (one or more) with different types of music to go with each exercise. Choose appropriate songs for each activity, having the remote or the CD player near you to change music. You will also need hand weights (small weights or heavy books, a rock, etc.). Have each person come prepared with work-out clothes and tennis shoes!

How to implement this study: Go through each physical activity as described in the chart and talk about how that activity works out or a particular part of the body and makes us strong (read the result in the middle column). Perform each activity for a few minutes, then stop and read the scripture and talk about how we can "spiritually" do the same exercise, which will result in strong spirits.

I Timothy 4:7,8 I have fought the good fight, I have finished the race, I have kept the faith. Now there is in store for me the crown of righteousness, which the Lord, the righteous Judge, will award me on that day – and not only me, but also to all who have longed for his appearing.

Action	Result	Verse
STRETCHING Stretch the arms, torso and legs to soft music.	Prevents Injury Prepares you for the race	Jude 20, 21, 24 Begin with faith, pray in the spirit, keep yourselves in God's love. This will prepare you for your spiritual race and protect you from injury.
RUNNING Run in place to some lively music.	Endurance	I Corinthians 9:24-27 You will run your whole life. Make sure the things you do have eternal value.
WEIGHTS Lift hand weights, or other weighted objects, while listening to a song of your choice.	Strength	Hebrews 12:11-12 Hard times will produce a harvest of righteousness and peace.
PUSH-UPS Perform different types of push-ups suited for each age, listening to music with a strong beat.	Arms that can praise God and lift up others	Psalms 18:31,32 When your arms become strong, help your neighbor.
LUNGES Stand up and lunge each direction, stretching those thigh muscles, continue with music.	Strong legs that won't stumble	Proverbs 4:12-14 As you walk along, make wise choices and obey God's commands and the instructions of your parents.
DANCING Allow free expressions here, to a song of worship.	Healthy heart That delights in God	Psalm 149:3,4 Always remain humble, giving praise to God for all good things.

Layers of Shame

This study helps us peel off all shame associated with sin.

Preparation: You will need a dark pair of sunglasses, a sock hat, a heavy dark coat and a pair of big baggy pants, all in a bag. Assign a narrator and three actors, one to play Jason, the main character of the story, one to play "shame" and the third to play "love".

How to implement this study: The character of Jason should be dressed nicely. As the narrator reads the story, the actions of "Shame" and "Love", as well as the actions of Jason, are italicized. "Shame" will pull out his "covering" one at a time as he puts them on Jason. "Love" will be humble and unassuming as he covers Jason with kindness.

Shame is a painful emotion resulting from an awareness of inadequacy or guilt. This means when someone sins and feels guilty for it, they feel shame. Or if someone feels like they are less than those around them, they feel shame. Shame makes a person feel uncovered. Therefore, when one feels uncovered, he tries to cover himself and his shame.

Let's read in Genesis where Adam and Eve covered themselves with fig leaves because they were ashamed. When Adam and Eve sinned, they became aware of their nakedness and tried to cover themselves. Sin brings shame to the sinner. ***Read Genesis 3:6-8.***

Narrator will read the story, while Shame sits in a corner with his bag. Love waits patiently on the sofa...

Jason is a nice young man, full of life and hope, and he has lots of friends. He even attends church on Sundays with his parents. However, some events in his life occur and Jason starts to pile on layer after layer of shame:

The first thing Jason did was start watching a lot of TV late at night while his parents were sleeping. (*Jason sits on the sofa and stairs at the TV*). He would stay up and flip channels, watching anything that looked good to his eyes. He knew certain things were not good to watch, and even harmful, but he was lazy and would not turn off the TV.

Jason felt guilty about this, but kept doing it. He began wearing big dark sunglasses everywhere he went, trying to look cool, but he was really ashamed of what his eyes has been watching. *(Shame places the dark glasses over Jason's eyes)*.

Jason started thinking about what he had been watching on TV late at night, and he would let his mind wander off. He had watched some late night ads about psychics foretelling the future of your life, and he was curious. He even began to look for books about fortune tellers at the library. It felt wrong to be thinking about this, but his curiosity got the best of him. *(Jason pretends to flip through pages)*.

Jason kept his books hidden under his bed, ashamed that he was reading them. He began wearing a big pullover cap, with his sunglasses. *(Shame sneaks up on Jason and slides the cap over his head)*.

Somehow, covering up his head made him feel less ashamed of what he had been thinking and reading about under the covers with his flashlight. He wore this cap every day, in the cold and the heat, as he didn't want his head exposed at all.

Jason's heart was getting cold, because now he was watching things on TV, reading harmful material and he began listening to music with hateful lyrics. He would put earphones in his ears and turn up the volume so loud he couldn't even hear anything else around him.

He even slept with the earphones in his ears and the music playing loud, while he was going to sleep at night. His heart grew colder and darker, until he began to act out in school and at home. *(Jason acts as if he is listening to music and moving to the beat).*

Jason felt alone and just wanted to hide. He began wearing a big black coat everywhere he went. *(Shame slips the dark coat over Jason and smiles as if to say "I've got him now.")*

It felt good to be covered up, because somehow he was always cold. Everything Jason was wearing so far was beginning to feel a bit heavy and it became a chore to get dressed each day. But he felt so dark and alone, these things became necessary for him to wear. He started hanging out alone, and shutting himself up in his room. He felt ashamed of himself, but he was so far into his routine, he didn't know how to get out.

In gym class the next day, Jason was dressing and another boy made fun of Jason's skinny legs. The boys all started calling Jason names, like "chicken legs", or "toothpick", and Jason was so embarrassed. *(Shame nips and picks at Jason's legs).*

Jason was ashamed to wear shorts anymore, and he began wearing long baggy pants, and refused to dress out in gym. *(Shame tosses Jason the baggy pants and Jason puts them on).* He got in trouble from the coach, but Jason would just sit in a corner and watch the other boys play. *(Jason sits against the wall with his legs drawn up).*

All of these layers he wore began to feel really heavy. Every day he put on his sunglasses, pulled on his sock cap, slipped into his heavy coat and baggy pants, and every day these things got heavier and heavier. These layers weighed him down and made him hang his head and walk in shame everywhere he went. Jason was a miserable young man, so deep in shame he could barely see the sidewalk in front of him.

(Jason gets up to walk, with his head hanging down and his feet dragging).

(NOTE: Obviously, not everyone who wears this type of clothing is full of shame, this is just a picture of how the feelings Jason has on the inside are reflected on the outside.)

Let's stop a minute and consider something:

Shame comes upon people in many ways. Shame can come from being disobedient, from participating in activities we know are wrong, from being embarrassed by others, etc. Shame is ugly and makes the person walking in shame want to hide. When a person is full of shame, they try to cover that shame with whatever they can find to hide under...

Read James 5:19-20. Love covers a multitude of sin.

Finally, another guy at Jason's school noticed Jason one day and invited him to sit with him at lunch. *("Love" brings Jason over to the table and sits down with him.)* Jason was apprehensive at first, but the guy was really nice. The next day Jason's pants fit a little better and he walked with a little bit of confidence. *(Jason takes off the baggy pants to reveal the pants that fit him. He tosses the baggy pants into Shame's lap.)*

Jason was walking home, and the same guy caught up with him and walked with him all the way to Jason's house. *(Love and Jason walk side by side)*. That guy didn't even live on the same street as Jason, but he walked with him anyway. Jason walked in the door of his house and took off his heavy black coat and got rid of it up for good. *(Jason tosses his black coat over the head of Shame.)*

Jason saw his dad's Bible lying on the table and decided to see what was so interesting that made his dad read it every day. He turned to **_Romans 10:11_**. *("Love" sits beside him while he reads the verse aloud.)*

He read a little more and realized that he was beginning to feel warm inside and outside, so he tossed his hat aside. *(Jason places his cap on the head of "shame".)*

That night after everyone was in bed, Jason turned on the TV. For some reason the same junk he had been watching seemed pointless tonight, so he turned it off. He went to sleep and had a really cool dream about winning a race. *(Jason lies down on the sofa and smiles)*.

The next morning Jason forgot his sunglasses, when he stepped out the door to walk to school. *(Jason places the sunglasses on the table, and Shame picks up the glasses and slouches back down in the corner, planning his attack on his next victim.)* Layer by layer, shame had fallen off of Jason. It all started with an act of kindness and love.

His steps were lighter, his head was higher and when he got to school, most kids didn't even recognize him. Jason felt covered in love and had no need to cover himself with shame.

Are there friends you know who might be full of shame, either from other kids teasing them or from bad decisions they have made? Do you sometimes feel ashamed?

Read Psalm 25: 3a (aloud together)
NO ONE WHOSE HOPE IS IN YOU WILL EVER BE PUT TO SHAME.

Make a decision that you won't walk in shame, and if you see another person with their head hanging down, you will be the love of God to them, by offering kindness and friendship.

LEAP OF FAITH

This study will help us believe God for BIG things.

Preparation: You will need the following: a big leaf, a penny, an imaginary line or a chalk line from which to jump, room to play leapfrog and a bed on which the whole family can sit. Write out the following words in large letters on different sheets of paper and place them around on the floor: Hatred, Murder, Abuse, Crime and Darkness.

How to implement this study: This study requires a family room with space to move about. Read the study and act out each activity, while exercising your faith together in prayer.

The phrase "leap of faith" is used when we say we are taking a big risk at something. Maybe a person is trying a new sport they never tried before and it requires a "leap of faith" that they will enjoy it and do well. Maybe a person is starting up a new business that requires lots of time and money, and they are taking a huge "leap of faith", hoping it will prosper and succeed. Anything that looks hard or requires lots of effort, or a huge miracle, requires a lot of faith. In this study, we are going to exercise our faith together, asking God for "big" things.

Leap of a leaf (*blow a leaf across the table and see where it lands*) – It doesn't take much to move a leaf and make it leap in the air. Just a little wind will do it, because a leaf is so light. Some things are easier than others to believe for. However, nothing is impossible to those who believe, if they pray according to His Word. Start your exercise in faith by praying for this study, for those participating to have their faith increased and stretched like never before (*have someone pray*).

Leap of a penny (*use your finger to flick or pop a penny across a table, and see who can flick it the farthest*). – The penny represents money. There are many financial needs in the world, from a single parent needing money for groceries, to the starving children in Africa needing a warm meal for their stomach. Exercise your faith and pray for huge financial blessings to fall on those who need it. Name anyone specifically that you can think of. *(Have each one call out a specific country or group of people and ask God to provide for their needs.*

Leap onto something and stomp on it (*leap onto the "evils" and stomp*) – There is evil present in this world because many people are full of hate and evil thoughts. Jesus is holy and pure and in His name we can take a leap of faith and stomp out the evil around us. (*After you stomp out the "evil", give thanks to God for his love and ask him to send his love to those who do evil things.*)

Leap of your body (*Stand from an imaginary line and see who can leap the longest jump*). Usually the taller the person, the longer the stride, the wider the arm swing, the longer the jump will be. Our bodies can do amazing things. However, many people are very ill, disabled and diseased, or tormented in their bodies so that they cannot function properly. If you know of someone like this, pray for their healing. (*Call out names or diseases and ask for healing to come to these people.*)

Leap Frog (*leap frog across each other as you exercise your faith*) – Leap frog requires energy on the part of the person leaping, and faith on the part of the person being leaped over, that the person leaping won't land on their back! Think of groups of people who need salvation, such as the homeless, the drug addicts, those who are full of hate, etc. and as you leap, call out these people and ask for salvation to come to them. Though it may look hopeless for some, nothing is impossible with God. Exercise your prayers by taking a giant leap of faith in an awesome God! (*Call out specific groups of people who seem to need a huge rescue from God.*)

Leap on the bed (*Be careful with this one...leap gently onto the bed, in a big pile*). Family and togetherness is very important. However, we live in a world where families are being redefined every day. Many kids don't even know who their parents are. Families are scattered around the nation, and togetherness is something many families don't ever experience. While you are piled together, pray and call out to Jesus for his healing presence in families of people you know and those you don't know. (*Ask Him to bring families together in His name.*)

Leap for joy (*Hold hands and leap for joy after praying*) – Finally, let's take a leap of faith and ask God for his joy to fill the earth. There are many sad and lonely people around us every day. We can bring God's joy to them through a smile, through and act of kindness, through a warm handshake, etc. Ask for joy to come to different groups of people and call them out, as you leap for joy. (*Call out groups such as the widows and widowers, the orphans, etc.*)

It is a good thing to exercise your faith by asking God for BIG things. We serve a big God and he hears all of our prayers. He is well able to do more than we can even think or ask. ***Read Ephesians 3:14-21.*** May God's faith dwell in us daily, and may we dare to believe him for the things we ask.

Let it Shine

This study teaches us ways we can let our light shine.

Preparation: This study will take place in the kitchen, around the table, preferably in the daytime. In the kitchen, (or nearby) you will need to have the following items for access: refrigerator, computer monitor (turned off), blinds or curtains that are shut, an unlit candle (with match lying beside it), a flashlight (with batteries out, lying beside it), oven and a lamp (with the switch on, but the bulb slightly unscrewed). Make a small circle of paper to fit over the end of the flashlight. Cut a star shape out of the middle and tape this to the end of the flashlight. Finally, have a fresh loaf of bread to break sitting inside the oven. (don't let anyone see this ahead of time)

How to implement this study: This study emphasizes letting our light shine, so as you read each scripture, let the light shine through each object listed above, and discuss the source of light.

Read Matthew 5:14-16

How does the light shine in the refrigerator? (*Have someone expose the light in the fridge.*) **It only shines when the door is opened**.

Acts 14:27 says the door of faith was opened to the Gentiles (unbelievers). When we exercise our faith through prayer and believing in God, we are opening the door for the light of God to shine on others.

How does the light show on the computer monitor? *(Have someone turn on the monitor)*. **It only shines when it is turned on**.

II Corinthians 4:6 says his light shines in our hearts to give us the glory of God. We must be "turned on" to Jesus in order for others to see the light.

How does a candle's light shine? *(Strike the match and light the candle)* **must be lit with fire**. Luke 3:16 says we can be baptized with Holy Ghost and fire. Pray that we are set on fire for Jesus so others can see us burn.

How does a flashlight shine? (*Place the batteries properly inside*) The batteries must be put in, **set in correct position**, in order for it to work.

Philippians 2:14, 15 says we need to be blameless and pure, without fault, so we can shine like stars as we hold out the word of life (*shine the flashlight and show a star on the ceiling*).

How does light shine in through windows? (*Open the curtains or blinds*) **That which was making it dark must be pulled aside.**

I John 1:5-7 states God is light and in him there is no darkness at all. We are to walk in the light, not sit in the dark. The light will draw others to him.

How does light shine through a lamp? (*Screw in the bulb*). The bulb must be screwed in and **securely tightened to the source** of electricity. Hebrews 6:19a says we have a hope that is an anchor for our soul, firm and secure. When we are secure in Him, others who are insecure will want what we have.

Finally, in order to see what's cooking inside an oven, we push a button to **turn on the light to see inside**. (*Push on the button to the oven and look inside, revealing fresh bread*). Sometimes friends or people we know can "push our buttons" and try to make us upset by talking about us behind our backs, calling us names, teasing, etc. Pray that when they push our buttons, the light that is inside shines through by our response to them, showing kindness and love instead of meanness and hate. In doing so, we can present them a freshly baked loaf of bread, hot and satisfying to all who taste.

Break bread together, praying that you will be a light to all those around you, bringing them to Jesus, the bread of life.

Little is Much

This study shows us how with God, anything is possible.

Preparation: You will need a bag of pinto beans uncooked, in the bag, unopened, and a clear bag of brown sugar, unopened. You will also need a big pan with sides, like a large cookie sheet or jellyroll pan, a red marker and a bag or container to use for transferring the sugar.

How to implement this study: Have this study around a table, where all can see what's going on. Set the pan in the middle and have the other items to the side. Read along and follow the directions in the study.

Read Judges 7:1. Gideon started into battle with 32000 men, all together and proud. *(place the bag of beans in the middle of the pan, wrapped in the covering, snug and secure).*

Read Judges 7: 2-3. God said that was too many men, so he ordered the ones who were afraid to turn back and leave. 22000 men left and 10000 remained. *(Open the bag and pour out about 2/3 of the beans into the pan, placing the discarded ones aside in the bag – these represent those who were afraid).*

Read Judges 7: 4-8. God said there was still too many men and told them to go to the water. Those who got a drink by lapping the water with their tongues like a dog were separated from those who knelt down and lapped with their hands. Those who lapped with their hands were chosen. *(Get rid of all but 9 beans left in the pan).*

Why did God do this?

1. He did not want the men to boast in their own strength. (He decreased their size).

2. He did not want fear among the men, for it would discourage those who were fighting. (He sent the fearful home).

3. He did not want those who looked away from the battle (showing they were not prepared) to fight. (He only wanted those who kept a watchful eye at all times.)

Now there were only 300 men left and God said he would give them the victory with these few good men.

Read Judges 7:9-12. The enemy was huge; their camels could not even be counted, as they were like sand on a sea shore! *(Place the bag of brown sugar (unopened) at one end of the pan, and 9 little beans at the other end of the pan)*.

Read Judges 7: 13-14. After Gideon heard about a dream where a loaf of barley bread (this was considered an inferior grain) tumbled into the enemy's camp and knocked over their tent, Gideon was encouraged and worshiped God.

Read Judges 7:15. He returned to his small group of men and told them that they would win the battle over the enemy. *(Place the nine beans in a circle, noting their unity)* This encouragement gave the men boldness and they obeyed everything Gideon said.

Read Judges 7:16-18. He divided the 300 into three companies, and placed trumpets and empty jars into their hands, with torches inside the jars. *(divide the beans into three groups of three).* The jars with torches symbolized the presence of God with them, and trumpets were going to be used to sound out deliverance. *(place a red mark on each of the nine beans, showing that they were set apart, on fire for God).*

Read Judges 7:19-23. When the men obeyed and the trumpets sounded, the Lord caused the men in the enemy's camp to turn on each other with their own swords. *(Place the nine beans so that they surround the bag of sugar).*

Read Judges 7:24-25. When the original men in Gideon's army heard of these great events, they returned and joined in the battle. *(Add back a few beans from the bag of those that had been discarded and place them around the sugar, sort of making a way around the "enemy").*

Read Judges 8:28. That enemy never bothered them again…the victory was won with a very small army of obedience, bold, trusting men. Little was definitely much, because of obedience to God. *(Slit open the sugar and transfer it to a sealed plastic bag or container, putting it away, and leave the empty open bag).*

Talk with your family about how "little is much" can be true for you personally. For example, some may feel little in size, little in faith, little in confidence, etc. Confess any areas where you may feel "little" and ask God to come and make you obedient, strong and mighty, overcoming every enemy you may face. Then worship God together and give praise to his name for his mighty power to overcome the enemies in our lives.

Open My Eyes

This study points to things around us and the need to really "see".

Preparation: This study requires a bit of setting up around the house: Place a dish towel and a bath towel in the dryer, make sure a trash can in the kitchen is full, mess up the pillows on the sofa and throw one on the floor, place a dirty dish in the sink, a backpack thrown in the doorway of a room, leave a light on in the bathroom and a refrigerated item sitting out on the counter.

How to implement this study: As you go through this study, you will be asking each person to perform a chore or task, and as they perform the chore, they have to observe the area and see if there's anything else they can notice that needs to be done. Discussion will follow.

This study teaches us to have "open" eyes to the world around us, so that when we go about our everyday business we see opportunities to a blessing to those we meet.

Tell the family that they will be asked to perform a task, and then they are to observe that area and see if there is another task that could be done in the same area. If they are unable to see the task or do it, help them out. Follow along below:

1. Ask someone to get a dish towel out of the dryer. *(When they get the dish towel out of the dryer, they should notice another towel in there, dry as well. They should fold this towel and put it away.)* A towel is mentioned in the Bible as a symbol of being a servant, in the story of Jesus washing the disciples' feet. God may put you in a situation where you can **"open your eyes"** and see a way to serve someone around you, while you are serving yourself. *(solicit examples, i.e. when you're at a party and you get a drink for yourself, offer to get one for someone else as well.) Read Galatians 5:13,14.*

2. Ask someone to throw away a piece of paper in the trash can in the kitchen. *(They should notice the trash is full and take it out).* Trash is something we get rid of, as we don't want it in our house. It's something we've thrown away. Let's make sure we **"open our eyes"** to things we don't need any more and be careful that we don't just hold on to things we don't use. Instead, we can give them to others in need. *(solicit examples of getting rid of old clothes, toys, etc.) Read I Timothy 6:17-19.*

3. Ask someone to sit on the sofa. *(They should notice the messed up pillows and arrange them on the sofa.)* Pillows bring comfort to those sitting on the sofa. When we are comfortable ourselves, and our lives are going well, ask God to **"open our eyes"** to see those around us who may be uncomfortable. We could offer a seat to someone who is standing or be a friend to someone who has just moved into our neighborhood. *(Solicit other examples). Read II Corinthians 1:3,4.*

4. Ask someone to get you a drink from the kitchen. *(They should notice the dirty dish in the sink, rinse it and put it in the dishwasher).* Sometimes we

leave a dish in the sink because we think it's just one dish and what will it hurt to just leave it in the sink. But if several dishes are left, it makes a big mess for someone else to have to take the time to rinse them and put them away. This is the same way with "small" sins that we think we'll deal with later. But we should never let anger, greed, hatred, etc. sit in our hearts. Let's **"open our eyes"** to see our faults, take these things to Jesus and let him make our hearts pure and clean again. (*Take a moment here to stop and pray...) Read Romans 6:11-13.*

5. Ask someone to enter the doorway of the room where the backpack has been thrown (*They should notice it and see that they have to step over it to enter, thus picking it up off the floor*). Sometimes we throw things on the floor wherever we are, not thinking that someone may stumble over that item later. This could cause someone serious injury, if they fall or turn their ankle because of our carelessness. We often do this sort of thing when we're tired. Sometimes, when we're tired spiritually we need to **"open our eyes"** and make sure we don't cause others to stumble. For example, being rude to our parents when a friend is visiting or yelling at our sister or brother out in the backyard, could cause those who hear us to "stumble" in their own walk with the Lord. (*Think of other things that could cause someone to stumble*). *Read I Corinthians 10:31-33.*

6. Ask someone to walk enter the room where the light has been left on, look around, then come back. Just tell them there was something left undone in that room. (*They should see the light is on and turn it off.*) Sometimes when we're in a hurry or not thinking, we leave on lights, leave doors open, etc. Turning off lights after we exit a room saves energy

and keeps our electric bill from being too high. This means we're being considerate of our parents and the money they spend. Let's ask God to "**open our eyes**" to see ways that we can be considerate and kind to the people who are in authority over us, like our parents, our teachers at church and school and the leaders of our country. *(Think of other examples).* *I Peter 2:17.*

7. Finally, have someone enter the kitchen to see if there's anything that needs to be done there. *(They should see the item left on the counter and put it where it belongs, in the refrigerator).* Often things are out of place in a room, and if left there too long, the item may spoil, especially if it belongs in the refrigerator. When we use an item we need to put it back where it belongs, so the next person can find it when they need it. Every item has its place where it belongs. We must "**open our eyes**" to see others when they appear to be displaced or alone. For example, the elderly, the ill, the lonely, all need to feel wanted and like they have a purpose in life. Let's be careful that we don't just ignore these groups of people, but instead pray for them, visit with them and bless them. *(Pray for a particular person who fits in this category). Read Psalm 68:4-6.*

Sometimes we will be going about our everyday lives, going to school, to the store, to church, walking in our neighborhood, etc., just doing what we do all the time. However, if we "open our eyes", God may just choose to show us something to do to bless Him in even the smallest of activities of our life. Open your ears and your eyes to be aware of your surroundings, blessing your family and others you meet.

Pass the Baton

This study talks about the race we are in, and the need we have to help one another.

Preparation: You will need a baton (you can make one out of toilet paper tube, just color the two ends of it with a black marker). Set up the following items around the house: a cup of water sitting on the kitchen table, an obstacle in the hallway, a dark closet, an uplifting song ready to be sung, and a hearty snack ready to be eaten together.

How to implement this study: Let one person begin the race with the baton and run in place. As they tire out, let another person take the baton and lead the first runner to the kitchen, for the first refreshing station. Let that runner run in place and as they tire, let another member take the baton and lead that runner to the sofa to rest, and so on. Keep passing the baton back and forth, helping each other along as you read the study below.

Did you know we are in a race? *Read I Corinthians 9: 24-27.* Just like in a marathon, we are runners together towards a goal. Along the way, we encounter all sorts of things, and we need each other to help us make it to our final destination.

Hand the baton to the first "runner" and let them "run" in place. This runner is running full steam ahead and is tired and thirsty. *Have the next runner lead the thirsty runner to the kitchen for the fresh cup of water. Read Prov. 11:25* and realize how refreshing it is to help a brother in need.

This new runner is tired and just needs a small resting place, before continuing on with the race. *Lead the runner to the sofa for a quick rest. While he's resting,* **read Isaiah 40:31** *to encourage this runner to be renewed in the strength of the Lord and hand the baton to the next runner.*

This runner has come to an obstacle in his path (in the hallway). Help him over it so he can continue the race. **Read Prov. 4:11, 12,** to encourage this runner that God will keep his feet from stumbling and have *the next runner take the baton.*

This runner has entered a dark place along the road (a dark closet) and is overcome with fear. Turn the light on so he can see the way to go, and **read Prov. 18:10** to encourage this runner that they can run to Jesus and feel safe. *Have the next runner take the baton and run.*

The runner is now just so weary that he cannot run any longer. He is too exhausted. *He falls down right in front of you and cannot get up on his own.* **Read Hebrews 12:1** to encourage this runner to fix his eyes on Jesus so that he can finish the race.

While the runner is resting and gaining back his strength, he is lead to a place of refreshing and hears sweet music. **Eph. 5:19** says to speak to one another in song. *Sing a song to this runner.*

Finally, those who have run the race together make it to the finish line and enjoy a huge feast and a big celebration for winning the race. **Read Rev. 19:9** and give thanks for the hope of heaven and enjoy your snack.

The Bible speaks of us being workers together, which means we don't run the race alone. We need each other. We need to be lifted up when we're tired, and we need to be there to encourage someone else when they need it.

Pass the baton when a friend is there to help you out, and take the baton from a friend so they too can rest.

PERCEPTION

This study helps us realize how everyone has a different "view" of things.

Preparation: You will need a pair of glasses, a scarf for a blindfold, a handheld mirror, an ice cube, and a plate of food with something on it that you know at least one person dislikes.

How to implement this study: This study needs to take place in a room where there is a door nearby, and a lamp available for use. Let someone read the lesson, while others act out each instruction in italics.

How you perceive or "view" things that happen in your life depends on your own personal experiences and your own self-esteem. For example, if you lose a dollar, perhaps you think it's no big deal. However, in a very poor country, losing a dollar could mean losing grocery money for a week! If you watch a game and you don't know anyone on the team or care about the game, and the team you're watching loses, who cares? However, if you are a key player on the team, and the losing the game means you're out of a chance to win a championship, losing the game can be disastrous! How we react to situations depends on how we perceive what is going on, and our perception can be different from person to person, depending on our own personal experiences.

(Have someone stand outside a door to a room, with the door barely open.) What can you see in the room? *(Have that same person now push the door open.)* What can you see now? When the door is barely open, you can only see a sliver of the room. When the door is wide open, you can see everything. This is how it is with our lives. We only see a small part of the world in our own neighborhoods.

We need to pray that God opens the door wider, so that we can see the world around us and the needs before us, so that we can effectively pray for everyone, not just our own little world.

Reading a book with poor eyesight and be painful. (*Have someone read either without their glasses that they normally wear, or with glasses that they don't normally wear.*) If your eyesight is poor, you need corrective lens. If your eyesight is good, using glasses you don't need makes your perception blurred and causes pain to your eyes. Reading the word of God without spiritual "glasses" will lead to boredom and may even make us fall asleep. We need to ask God to give us spiritual perception when we read, so that his word becomes alive in our hearts, not dull words to our ears.

(*Blindfold a person and instruct them to walk across the room and pick up a coin.*) If your vision is covered up from something someone has tied around your face, you can't see at all where you're going and can only guess or feel your way around. A non-Christian is blind spiritually. It's like a veil (covering) is over their eyes. They cannot see where to go, they have no purpose in life and if they hang around all non-Christians, they are like the blind leading the blind! Their perception is just what they see in front of their eyes, and that is darkness. They need someone to remove the blinders and show them the way. That someone could be us! (*Remove the blindfold and the person can see clearly where the coin lies.*) *Read II Corinthians 3:16-18 and II Corinthians 4:4.*

(*Turn off the lights and ask someone to read something. Turn on the lights and see how important the light is, when reading or following instructions or doing pretty much anything!*) Once the blinders have been removed, a person needs the light to illuminate their path so they can see where they're going. We who walk in the light, need to be aware that those who don't walk in the light cannot possibly see the way. We should not get mad or hurt at people who don't know Jesus, when they hurt our feelings or exhibit poor behavior. Instead, we should pray for them and let the light of God shine from our hearts into their hearts.

(*Place a plate of food in front of everyone.*) Does everyone see it as a plate of food they want to eat? (*Have each one answer if they would eat the food or not.*) Each person has his or her own individual tastes, dislikes and likes. For one person, the plate may make them so hungry that they grab the food and gobble it down. For another person, they may turn away in disgust, because they've tasted that particular food before and hated it. What you've tasted before determines what you're willing to taste now. Some people have "tasted" very bad things in life and it makes them afraid of others, or afraid of trying new things. Be patient, loving and kind if you know someone like this. Maybe they had a friend who betrayed them, so they're afraid of making new friends. Maybe their parents abandoned them, so they don't trust adults.

Look in the mirror. (*Let each one describe what they see about themselves, and then let each one describe what they see in the others.*) Some may focus on the hair, others on the eyes, and still others on the whole picture. We all have different perceptions of ourselves, how we see ourselves and how we "think" others see us. We must love ourselves before we can love others. Jesus loved us so much that he died for us. Don't let your self image be determined by anything in this world. You were made in the image of God and you are beautiful! When you realize this truth, you are free to see others as God's creation and you can love them, too. *Read Matthew 19:18.* To love our neighbors as ourselves means we must love ourselves. We cannot reach out to others if we don't see ourselves as being loved by God.

(See how long each person can hold an ice cube.) A person with tough skin may be able to hold it the longest. Others may have skin that is very sensitive to cold and may drop the ice immediately. One's perception of what is cold differs from another. You may wear a coat on a day that someone else feels no need for a coat. You may carry an umbrella when it's sprinkling outside and others may not mind getting a little wet. It's all in your own perception. Some people do well under pressure and it makes them just work harder. Others crumble under pressure and need relief. Be careful that you don't judge others, just because of how they react to pain, stress or difficult times. Pray for them.

(Look up into the sky and count the stars.) If it's cloudy, you can't even see the stars. What if you had a telescope? You could see lots of stars and maybe a planet! God has vision to see beyond what we can ever see with any kind of instrument or eyesight. Our vision is limited to a few feet in front of us. His vision is not limited at all, and he sees the whole picture. *Read II Corinthians 4:18.*

This study is to help us realize that people perceive life, things that happen to them, good or bad, in different ways, depending on their background, their home life and their own personal experiences. We also perceive life on this earth through human eyes, when God perceives our life through his wise, all-knowing, caring eyes, with an eternal purpose in mind. When we realize that our perception is not always what others perceive, and that what we perceive is not even what matters for all eternity, we can relax and accept life a little easier and accept others and their differences a little more. God has a plan, he sees the whole view, and we only see a small sliver of our lives here on earth. One day he will open the door and invite us in where we can see the whole picture, too. Can you imagine it? Can you even take it all in? One day all the little things that aggravate us about others and the way they view things won't matter, because we will all be face to face with God and all see clearly what it was he was trying to get us to see all the years we spent on earth.

God loves us, and he loves others. God made us and he made us all uniquely different. God sees all and we only see a little. We can trust him to guide us and we can trust him to use the different perceptions of people around us to sharpen us, make us more compassionate, mature us and bring us closer to him, if we will let him.

Popping

In this study we will make popcorn and learn awesome spiritual truths.

Preparation: You will need a popcorn maker or large pan with a lid, oil, popcorn for popping (if you can find it, use colored popcorn), salt and butter.

How to implement this study: Popcorn has many interesting facts about it that can be applied to our lives as Christians. Read the questions below and see if the kids know the answers. Go over each question and answer. Make some popcorn together, making note of the things you just learned, then sit down and enjoy the popcorn and a good movie together.

Read Galatians 3:26-29

We are the seed of Christ, scattered out in the world, to "pop" for him and bring a good "taste" to all those around us, so that when they taste and see, they too will want to know Christ.

1. **Does popcorn taste good as a seed**? No, it is too hard to bite and has no **flavor**. (*Let each one feel the seed and see that it is too hard to bite or chew.*) We are hard and tasteless too, until we come to know Jesus.

2. **What makes popcorn pop?** When the popcorn kernel is heated, the water inside the kernel heats and the pressure builds up. This causes the water to expand and the kernel pops or bursts. *John 7:37* says we have streams of living water inside us, when we have Jesus living in our hearts. *(Look closely at the seeds)* Do they look like they have water inside? How amazing that water is inside that tiny seed!

WATER MUST BE PRESENT INSIDE EACH SEED.

3. **Why is heat needed to make the kernel pop?** There must be a source of fire or heat to make the water expand, to cause the kernel to pop. **Heb. 12:28, 29** says our God is a consuming fire. *(Place the pan on the stove or plug in the popper.)*

FIRE MUST HEAT UP THE WATER INSIDE THE SEED.

4. **What else is needed for popcorn to pop**? Oil. The kernels have to spin in the oil, and be evenly coated with the oil and constantly be moving in the oil, before they will pop. **Isaiah 61:3** says he gives us the oil of gladness instead of sadness.

OIL (JOY) MUST SURROUND EACH SEED

5. **Why do some kernels not pop**? The ones that don't pop are called "old maids" and they don't pop because they are too dry. *(Pour in the oil and the seeds, and turn on the heat.)*

DRY KERNELS DON'T POP

6. Can the dry kernels be used? Only if they are soaked in water for several days. Wow, amazing! Even if we are dry sometimes, if we soak in the rain of God's love, we can become useful and tasty again!

WATER MUST BE PRESENT

7. Why do we salt and butter the popcorn? For flavor. It is best to eat the popcorn right away before it gets soggy and cold. **Matt. 5:13** says we are the salt of the earth. (Pour out the popcorn in a bowl and salt to taste, adding butter flavoring if desired.)

SALT MAKES IT TASTE GOOD

<u>Interesting fact</u>: Popcorn comes in all colors, from white to light gold, red, black, etc. We are all different "colors" to the world, but God uses each and every one of us in our own unique way.

Did you learn something new about popcorn? Always allow yourself to be full of the water of the Spirit, the heat of the love of God and the oil of joy and gladness, and you will find yourself hopping around, popping out goodness and flavor to everyone around you.

Pray together that you will allow the fire of God to heat up the living water within you, so that you will spin around in the oil of joy and explode into something tasty for all the world to see and enjoy, Jesus Christ, who lives in you.

Pulling together

In this study, we will see the need for every person in our lives.

Preparation: Have these items scattered around the room, easy to find: State or Country map with a highlighter, paper and pencil, any snack, umbrella and blanket, flashlight and jumper cables, band-aids and cold medicine, and a camera. Make sure everyone has a copy of the fill-in-the-blank section of this study.

How to implement this study: As you gather the items for the road trip, make sure <u>everyone</u> in the group has a part, so that no one is left out. The key is to make sure every person participates. Place the map and highlighter on the table to begin.

When we all pull together, how happy we'll be…remember that song? (*Sing it, if you know the tune*).

> *When we all pull together, together, together,*
> *when we all pull together how happy we'll be,*
> *for your work is my work and our work is God's work.*
> *When we all pull together, how happy we'll be."*

Did you know that our journey on this earth is like going on a road trip? Did you know that this road trip is a lot more fun and a lot less hazardous if you and the others on the trip with you pull together your resources, knowledge and skills? Traveling on a road trip alone can be very long and tiring, as well as boring, and could even be dangerous. Why do we all need to pull together? It is because we are all different people with different gifts and different personalities, all working together for a common goal, living a life for Christ, sharing his love with others and making heaven our home.

When you begin a trip, you need a destination and a map with directions on how to get there. (*Open the map and choose a place from the brochures that you would like to visit that is far from your home, a place you can drive to, and circle your home city and that city.*)

Someone needs to be willing to drive, and that someone needs to be skillful at driving, alert and trustworthy, and must have a valid license to drive! (*Designate the person who will be the driver and talk about why that person should drive.*)

We need to know why it is that we're going to our chosen destination! What is there that we want to see? We need some excitement for this trip! (*Discuss why you chose the spot you want to visit. Who has heard about the place and what there is to do and see there? Have someone convince the others that this place is a good choice.*)

What is the cost of this trip? (*Ask the person who handles the money if they have any idea.*) How will the family save the money to go? *(Let person make a list of probable expenses.)*

Food will be needed for the trip. (*Decide on the person in the family who should be responsible for getting the food together, and discuss why you pick that person. Eat the snack provided)*

Along the road, there might be inclement weather, so we need to be prepared. We might encounter extreme temperatures or drive through stormy weather. We don't want to get stuck and be miserable, if the weather turns bad! *(Have another person get the umbrella and a blanket.)*

The vehicle we are driving could break down, just due to wear and tear, so we should have a few tools *(Let someone get a flashlight and jumper cables).*

A first-aid kit is essential when packing for a long road trip, just in case we get a cut or get a cold. *(Let another person go find the Band-aids and some cold medicine.)*

One thing we want to be sure to have is good camera. We want to capture the moments and the places we see along the way, so we can share them with others we know and love. *(Get the camera and decide who should take most of the pictures and why...)*

We are all "pulling together" our resources for the trip, choosing each one to take part in the journey. If we tried to make this long trip alone, we would become tired and weary, we would have no one to help if we encountered trouble and there would be no one with whom we could share the beautiful sights we see. Let's compare our "road trip" and pulling together to our "heavenly trip" and pulling together. Fill in the blanks with as many different people/groups/ places as possible. Try not to repeat an answer in any blank.

You have a destination at the end of your life. Where will it be? _____.
You need a driver, someone who knows the way and can get you there safely. Who would that be? _____.
Who told you about heaven? _____What have you heard about it? _____

_____.

Who will pay for this trip?_____. What does it cost? _____.

Along the way, you might get thirsty and hungry. Where will you get food and drink for your soul? _____.

What people whom you know are good at providing shelter and safety from storms in your life?_____.

If you get discouraged and "break down" who could you turn to for help? _____

When your feelings are hurt or you just need some comfort, who gives that comfort to you? _____.

Who are the friends that you love to share memories with, and you love to have with you along the way? _____ _____.

Hopefully, Jesus is your "driver" and companion along this trip. But hopefully, you have other people in your life that pull together with you, to make your journey pleasant, safe and on the right path. It takes everyone doing their part, using their gifts and abilities, to make our journey one to be remembered. Some are good at cheering us on, others are good at feeding our soul, a few friends are good at listening to our hardships, and still others are good at encouraging us when we're down. Give thanks for each one and remember, "When we all pull together, how happy we'll be."

Finally, read I Thess. 4:16-18, 5: 11, 14-18 and 28.
Encourage each other, pull together your individual resources/gifts and make your journey joyful and complete. *(All together, put away all the things you took on your "trip").*

*P*ut your best foot forward

This study involves observing feet, beautiful feet!

Preparation: Have a large basket or bowl with the following items in it: warm, wet, rolled-up washcloths for each person, a bottle of lotion and a pair of socks for each person. Also place each person's tennis shoes in front of them. If you have time, plan this study so that you can take a family walk afterwards.

How to implement this study: Have each person come barefoot to this study. Follow along with the directions below.

Observe the feet of those around you. How are they different? How are they the same? Feet are all different. Some people have long, skinny feet, some have short little toes, and some feet are just plain smelly! **Isaiah 52:7** says that the feet which bring good news are beautiful. *(Take time to tell each other how beautiful their feet are when they spread the good news of Jesus.)*

Feet often get dirty, either because of wearing sandals all day, or from walking barefoot around dirty floors. In Bible days, the people wore sandals, so their feet were very dirty by the end of the day. **John 13:5** says Jesus began to wash his disciples' feet. What a beautiful act of love. *(Take a warm, wet cloth and wash each other's feet.)*

When we see the "walk" sign on the street, we know it's safe to cross. God directs our footsteps. **Read Psalm 119:105 and 133**. He knows when we need to stop and rest, he knows when our feet are tired, he knows everything about our walk with him, and he gently guides us along. *(rub lotion on your tired feet)*.

Socks are placed on our feet for comfort and covering. *(put on socks)* **Prov. 4:27** says he will keep our feet from evil. When we choose to follow Jesus, he protects us from the evil one. Socks feel warm and cozy when it's cold, and staying next to Jesus feels warm and cozy, too.

Psalm 121:3 says he will keep our feet from slipping. **Heb. 12:13** says he makes level paths for our feet. This indicates that we might sometimes have to walk in slippery places, or climb up hills. We often wear tennis shoes when we want good traction while we walk, as indicated in this picture. This verse proclaims God's protection over us and how he gives us his strength to do what he has called us to do. We also gain our strength from reading his word and praying. *(Take time now to exercise your feet – rotate your feet, bend them back and forth and wiggle your toes, then put on your tennis shoes.)*

Matt. 22:44 and **Rom. 16:20** says God puts Satan under our feet. This means he gives us his authority to crush and destroy wrong ideas, thoughts and actions that come into our mind. We don't have to listen to the devil and his lies. *(Stand up and stomp in your tennis shoes, thanking God for conquering evil)*.

The hands, the feet and every part of your body are all important. Your hands are not more important than your feet, and your feet are not more important than your hands.

Every part of the body is unique and useful, just like every part of God's body is unique and useful. Read **I Cor. 12:21** and see what the Bible says about this. *(stand up and hold hands with your family, each one giving thanks aloud for the person next to them).*

Psalm 40:2 says he sets our feet upon a rock. When we follow him, stay close to him, stomp on evil and let him cleanse us daily, we will stand firm on the rock beneath us, Christ Jesus our Savior and Lord.

(Take a walk with your family, observing God's goodness in nature and thanking him for beautiful feet)

Reaction

This study looks at the reasons behind reactions.

Preparation: Copy and cut out each numbered instruction on the last page and hand them out to partners for charades. You will need a book or object to be dropped, a creative piece by someone in the group (artwork or craft), a bag of opened pasta or beans and a piece of notebook paper that is folded up like a letter to be mailed.

How to implement this study: Each paragraph below has a "charade" for two people to act out to demonstrate each concept. As you go through each charade, notice the action and reaction going on. Talk about what the expected reaction is, and what really happens, and then read the coordinating paragraph and scriptures in the lesson.

Every day we do things, hoping, expecting and assuming a certain reaction from our actions. We get up and put our feet on the floor, expecting our legs to walk and hold us up. We turn on the faucet to brush our teeth and expect that the water will flow. We get in the car and turn the key, expecting the motor to start. We study hard for a test at school, expecting to get a good grade. All day long we act and we get a reaction, hopefully a reaction we want and expect. Then what happens? We get home from school and call a friend over to play, expecting them to react with joy and say yes. Instead, our friend says they have homework and their mom won't let them come. The next day we hear that our friend went over to another person's house and played with them instead. Oh no! Not the reaction we had hoped for, right?

Let's look at some more examples: (*Begin the charades now, each one being performed before you read the paragraphs and the scriptures.*)

1. When you offer a smile, it makes you feel good if the other person smiles back. When someone smiles at you, do you return the smile? God smiles on us every day we live, by giving us breath, food and shelter, and numerous other ways. Do you smile back and give him a nod? (*Read Psalm 40:5*). God gives us blessings every day, too many to count. The least reaction we can give him a big smile from our heart.

2. Giving thanks should be a normal reaction for nice things people do for us. A grateful heart must be in the heart of every believer. When the Lord blesses you with the good things in life, and carries you through the bad times in life, you must always remember to react with thanksgiving. (*Read Luke 17:11-19*). Ten were healed, but only one reacted with thanksgiving. Make sure you are like that one.

3. When you've worked hard on a project, you want some type of recognition for it. When others praise your efforts, your talents and your abilities, it makes you feel good about yourself. Think how you would feel if you created a masterpiece that took you a year to complete, you hung it up in your room for your friends to see and enjoy, and yet they come in and keep their heads to the ground, never noticing what you have created. Our God has created a beautiful sky, colorful scenery and awesome human beings that we are around every day. Take notice. React. (*Read Psalm 148:1-6*).

4. Wouldn't it be so frustrating if you noticed a dirty kitchen sink full of dishes, you cleaned them and put them away, and the rest of the family never noticed. What if they just

came in the kitchen and filled it with dirty dishes again, just minutes after you cleaned up? Did you know that God comes in and fixes the messes in our lives over and over again? Do we stop and take notice? Or do we just get in a mess again? When we sin, our reaction should be to ask forgiveness and ask for strength to resist the temptation to sin again. (*Read I John 1:9*).

5. Suppose you took the time to write a letter to a dear friend telling them how much they mean to you. How would you feel if that friend never said a word about the letter and never responded back with a letter to you? God has written books of love letters to us. Our reaction should be at the very least to read them. However, if we read them and believe them, we will react with love letters and love prayers back to our God. (*Read Revelation 1:3*).

6. When everyone is talking at one time in a big room, it just sounds like noise. When a teacher talks in front of a class, some kids sleep or tune them out. When a parent is disciplining their child, the kid sometimes reacts with anger and refuses to listen. Do we react with respect and honor when God talks? He talks to us through his word, through our leaders at church, through nature, etc. Are we listening? (*Read James 1:22*).

7. Wouldn't it be silly if you asked a friend how to get to their house, and you headed out in the opposite direction? That would be absurd! Jesus is the ONLY way to heaven, the ONLY way to peace and joy, and yet so often we react to his direction by turning and walking away from him. (*Read John 14:6*).

How will you react to this bible study? Pray together that God will make you more aware of your reactions to others around you and to the blessings of God in your lives.

1. One person smiles at the other person, but that person just looks away and frowns, ignoring the smile.

2. One person drops something, the other person hands it to them. The person who dropped it just grabs it and goes on, without saying anything.

3. Display a creative piece to your friend, and the friend just makes a face and goes on about their business.

4.   One person spills the bag of beans or pasta (only a few!), and the other person picks them up. The first person spills them again, over and over.

5.   One person takes a letter, writes the other person's name at the top and hands it to them. The person receiving the letter just tosses it aside, not reading a word.

6. One person begins a conversation with the other person. The person who is supposed to be listening just hums and taps their feet, not listening at all.

7. One person gives the other person a direction by pointing a certain way to go. The other person turns and goes the opposite direction.

Read the Label

In this study, we will read the labels and get to know what's inside.

Preparation: Find the following items and lay them out on a tray: Item with label "made in China", item with label "dry clean only", jar of peanut butter, something with an expiration date on it, medicine bottle with label, a piece of fruit with a label (like a banana), a movie and a computer disk that is labeled.

How to implement this study: Before beginning, ask if anyone can guess what all of the items have in common (labels). Discuss how we must read labels on everything, or we can really get in trouble. Let each one read the label and then the question, and fill in the blank. In the same way, we must read God's labels (instructions) to us in his word.

Made in China

This label tells you where the help came from to make this item. Read the Bible's label and where does your help come from?_____
Psalm 121:1,2.

Dry clean only

This label tells you how to clean an item in the best possible manner. Read the label in the Bible and write down how we are made clean._____
_____ Psalm 51: 1,2.

INGREDIENTS…peanuts

This label lets you know that one of the ingredients used is peanuts. If you are allergic to peanuts, you know not to eat this food, as it will make you sick. Who in the Bible was warned not to eat a certain thing? _____ _____Gen. 2:17 . What happened when they did?_____ _____.

Expires 12/07

This label lets you know that you need to use the product before the expiration date. After that, it is no good. There is a time for everything, a time to laugh, a time to cry, a time to plant, etc.. Read Ecc. 3:1. Write it down.

_____

_____

Take 2 tsp. every four hours

This label's instructions must be followed exactly, in order to regain your health and be well. Read Prov. 16:20. What will happen to those who follow God's instructions? _____.

DOLE

This label tells you the name of the company who manufactured the fruit. The company places their label on the fruit, signifying it is good. If the fruit is bad, it reflects badly on the name. Prov 22:1 says a good name

is more desirable than what?_____
We bear the name of Jesus as Christians, and we must be
a good reflection of his character.

Rated PG

The label on a movie lets you know the kind of content in
the movie and what age group should watch it. What is
the Bible rated? In other words, who is it for? Read John
3:16 _____.

2HD IBM
1.4 mb

A computer disk only holds what is stored on it. What
are you storing? Matt 6:19,20_____
_____

R – E –S – P – E – C- -T

Showing respect is the theme of this study.

Preparation: Assign readers and actors for the story below. Have the story take place in a room with a window. Provide a sack lunch (just a snack inside), a few empty boxes, a pair of shoes behind a chair, a TV, a basketball, and a chocolate bar as props for those acting out the story.

How to implement this study: Read the story and have the actors interact with each other as you read. Follow the instructions in italics at the end of the story.

Read Hebrews 13:15-17 and I Thes. 5:12, 13

Respect is a feeling of appreciation and honor for someone for who they are or what they have done. The following story highlights some of the people who deserve our respect and honor. Notice the contrast between the characters of Ray and Dory.

Respectful Ray began his day as he always did. He got up, looked out the window and thanked **God** for a beautiful day to live. He was glad to be alive. He was thankful for those around him. He was sleepy and tired and wanted to go back to bed, but he knew it was his **mom**'s birthday, so he hurried to her room to give her a hug. He was whistling a tune he didn't even know, but it sounded good to him.

DISRESPECTFUL DORY BEGAN HER DAY AS SHE ALWAYS DID. SHE GOT UP AND HATED TO SEE THE MORNING. SHE SAW THE SAME VIEW OUT HER WINDOW THAT RAY DID, AS SHE LIVED NEXT DOOR. ONLY SHE WASN'T THANKFUL, SHE WAS MAD. SHE HAD PRAYED THAT **GOD** WOULD HELP HER ON HER FITNESS TEST AT SCHOOL YESTERDAY AND SHE FAILED IT. DORY FAILED IT BECAUSE SHE HAD NOT PRACTICED ANY OF THE DRILLS, BUT SHE WAS **ANGRY AT GOD** FOR NOT ANSWERING HER PRAYER. SHE MUTTERED UNDER HER BREATH AS SHE GOT DRESSED, "WHY BOTHER PRAYING...GOD DOESN'T LISTEN OR CARE."

Ray's dad was about to leave when Ray noticed his **dad** carrying several items and couldn't get the front door open. Ray quickly ran to the door and opened it for his dad. Dad smiled and thanked Ray. Ray went even further and helped his dad carry some of the items to his car. "Love you, Dad!" Ray said as he walked back to the house.

DORY ONLY LIVED WITH HER MOM, BECAUSE HER PARENTS WERE DIVORCED. DORY'S MOM WORKED HARD AT TWO JOBS TO HELP PAY FOR THE DANCE AND MUSIC LESSONS DORY TOOK AFTER SCHOOL. HOWEVER, MOST DAYS DORY WAS STILL ANGRY AT HER MOM FOR NOT BUYING HER THE NEW DANCE SHOES LIKE ALL THE OTHER GIRLS HAD. DORY'S MOM COULDN'T FIND HER SHOES THIS MORNING AND ASKED DORY TO HELP HER. DORY JUST **IGNORED** HER MOM AND QUICKLY RAN OUT THE DOOR, SO SHE WOULDN'T BE LATE TO WALK TO SCHOOL WITH HER FRIEND, SARAH.

Ray got to school, the same school where Dory attended. The bell rang and class began. The teacher turned on the

TV and the **President** was speaking. The teacher asked the class to listen for 15 minutes, and then she would ask them questions afterwards. Ray listened attentively, even though he didn't really understand all that the President was saying. He knew the President held the highest office in the land and he deserved to be listened to.

DORY WAS IN RAY'S CLASS AND SHE TOO HEARD THE PRESIDENT SPEAKING. DORY CHOSE TO WRITE NOTES AND CHEW GUM, MAKING COMMENTS ABOUT HOW STUPID IT IS FOR THE PRESIDENT TO WEAR A SUIT ALL THE TIME ON TELEVISION. SHE TUNED HIM OUT COMPLETELY, HUMMING SONGS IN HER HEAD FROM THE RADIO. WHAT A WASTE OF TIME, SHE THOUGHT, LISTENING TO THE PRESIDENT. WHO CARES WHAT HE HAS TO SAY? **IT WASN'T IMPORTANT TO HER**.

Respectful Ray tried his best to listen to his **teacher** throughout the day. His mom had been a teacher for a while, and he had watched her grade papers at night, worry about specific kids and still she had time to make Ray dinner and help him out with his own homework. Being a teacher was a hard job. He didn't really like homework, but he was thankful for the opportunity to learn. He had heard last week about children in other countries who don't even get to go to school.

DORY **TOOK EVERYTHING IN HER LIFE FOR GRANTED**. THIS MEANS SHE JUST ASSUMED EVERYTHING IN LIFE WAS OWED TO HER AND SHE SAW NOTHING IN HER LIFE OF ANY VALUE. SHE SAW HER TEACHER AS A MEAN OLD LADY WHOSE JOB IT WAS TO MAKE HER LIFE DIFFICULT. SHE DIDN'T NEED TO BE TAUGHT, AND BESIDES, HER TEACHER HAD A WEIRD ANNOYING VOICE

AND SOMETIMES TALKED TOO MUCH. MOST OF THE CLASS, DORY DOODLED AND HUMMED, **NOT LISTENING** AT ALL, THUS CAUSING THE TEACHER TO CORRECT HER SEVERAL TIMES.

Lunch came very soon and Ray was super hungry. He waited his turn and sat down to eat. He chewed quietly and kept his space clean. He talked with his **friends** and really listened to what they had to say. Ray had lots of friends because he was a good friend to them.
DORY SAT IN A SEAT DOWN THE TABLE FROM RAY AND SHE WAS LOUD. SHE RIPPED OPEN HER LUNCH SACK AND ELBOWED THE GIRL SITTING NEXT TO HER. "MOVE!" DORY'S **RUDE VOICE** DEMANDED. DORY SMACKED LOUDLY WHEN SHE ATE AND SPILLED TRASH ON THE FLOOR NEXT TO HER SEAT. MOST OF THE KIDS AROUND HER JUST TOLERATED DORY'S BEHAVIOR AND COULDN'T WAIT FOR LUNCH TO BE OVER. THE ONLY TALKING SHE DID WAS **GOSSIPING** AND SPREADING RUMORS SHE HAD HEARD ABOUT RAY, THE LITTLE "GOOD BOY" IN THE CLASS.

After school, Ray began to walk home. He knew some kids had spread a nasty rumor about him today, but he knew it wasn't true, so he didn't let it bother **him.** He was proud of his good grades and of the clothes he had to wear, and he wasn't going to let a nasty rumor spoil his day. Besides, his friends were waiting for him to shoot some baskets.

AFTER SCHOOL, DORY WALKED HOME ALONE. SARAH HAD DECIDED TO WALK WITH SOMEONE ELSE BECAUSE DORY HAD MADE HER MAD TODAY. DORY STOPPED AT THE CONVENIENCE STORE AND SPENT HER ALLOWANCE ON A HUGE COKE AND A CHOCOLATE CANDY BAR. SHE KNEW CAFFEINE MADE HER CRAZY, BUT HER MOM WASN'T AROUND TO SCOLD HER, SO SHE **DISOBEYED**

WHAT SHE KNEW TO BE RIGHT AND ATE WHAT SHE WANTED. WHO CARED? IT TASTED GOOD.

As Ray started home from playing with his friends, he met Dory on the road. She had been at the park too, watching the boys play basketball. Ray walked past Dory and came to a red light. He and Dory waited for their turn to walk. An <u>elderly</u> gentleman walked up with a cane. The man was hot and looked tired. Ray had an unopened bottle of water in his bag and he offered it to the man. Dory noticed. The old man smiled and thanked Ray. As they crossed the street, Dory saw Ray and for a moment she wished she could be like him. He always seemed to be happy. She felt bad that she had talked about him today. He really seemed like a nice kid. Ray turned around and waved at Dory as he turned on his street. Dory smiled and waved back. He noticed me, she thought. Dory walked in the door and called to her mom, "Can I help you with dinner?"

If you look back through the story of Ray, the underlined words show the people we should respect and honor. If you look at the story of Dory, the underlined phrases show the ways we disrespect or dishonor. Try to see where you could improve and ask God to help you have an honoring, respectful heart.

Resting....ahhhh.....

We will learn in this study about the need for rest.

Preparation: You will set up stations in the yard and around the home, ahead of time: a nice shaded area in the yard, with a blanket or chairs and pitcher of water and glasses, with some books and a Bible scattered around (for the sitting, reading, drinking and looking area); some candles ready to be lit in a room in the house (for the prayer and meditation time), and some pillows laid out on a bed or on the floor (for the sleeping area.)

How to implement this study: Just move through the different positions of rest as indicated below, and read the scriptures, discussing each position and why we need to rest. Generate questions from to family and find out their likes/dislikes about the different positions of rest.

*(Start out under the shade tree, sitting in chairs or on a blanket).***Sitting** *(Read SS 2:3, 4)* – Sitting gives your legs a rest from going and going, all the time. Sitting gives you time to be still and think. Sitting under a shade tree on a hot summer day is so refreshing. It gets you out of the sun and under a covering, where you can feel the breeze blow.

Something to try: Offer someone your seat next time you're in a crowded place.

Reading*(Give each one a book or the Bible to read for a few minutes. You may want to bookmark an area to read, or let them choose) (Read Psalm 62:1, 2)* – Reading relaxes your mind and gets you to stop thinking of all the things you have to do or places you have to go, and lets you "escape" a while. Just make sure what you are reading is good for your mind and soul.

Something to try: See if you can find the age of the youngest king in the Bible (his name is Josiah).

Looking *(look at the plants and trees and observe their beauty)*–Observing things around you makes you stop and give thanks. *(Read Gen. 2:2,3.)* After God created the world, he rested, not because he was weary, but to observe what he had made and how complete and perfect it was. We need to rest and observe how complete and perfect we are in God's sight and to observe what a beautiful, wonderful world he has made.

Something to try: Next time you look in the mirror, take a long gaze at your face and how perfectly made and beautiful it is. Give thanks to God for giving you life.

(take a drink of cool water together) **Drinking** – taking a break to have a cool drink on a hot day is so refreshing. *(Read John 7:37)* – Letting yourself get too thirsty when you are hot, can result in dehydration. You can become ill and pass out if you get too dehydrated. The same thing happens to your soul if you go too long without a drink from the "living" water.

Something to try: Mix 4 large strawberries, ½ cup milk, 1 banana, 5 ice cubes in a blender until smooth. Add 1 ½ t sugar and blend one minute. This makes a refreshing smoothie!

(now move inside the house to a room and light the candles)

Praying –*(Read Phil. 4:6, 7)* Praying gives rest to your soul, you can give God all your worries and fears and trust him to take care of your life. Praying is also being obedient to God, because he says to pray always and to pray in faith.

Peace comes to those who pray. *(Have one person pray aloud, giving all the cares of life over to Jesus...)*

Something to try: Next time you pray, use your five fingers to pray: thumb (it points to you, so pray for forgiveness of any sins in your heart), first finger (it points to others, so pray for friends you know who are not saved), middle finger (it is the biggest, so pray for the leaders of your country), ring finger (it represents family, so pray for your parents and brothers and sisters), and little finger (since it's the weakest, pray for those you know who are sick).

Meditating – *(Read Psalms 119:15, 16; 23, 24; 27; 78; 95; 97; 148)* (*Let each one read aloud as they find each verse about meditating.*) Meditating requires resting and pondering, and it builds faith. Thinking on one verse or one passage from the bible can fill your spirit with new life and new energy.

Something to try: Think of one adjective that describes God and meditate on that for two full minutes (examples: wonderful, mighty, loving, awesome, etc.)

(now move to the room where the pillows have been placed)

Sleeping – *(Read Psalm 127:2)* – Sleeping gives your whole body rest so that you can be renewed when you awake. Your body is not designed to go without sleep. While you sleep, you grow, you dream, you heal, etc. All sorts of things happen while you're not even awake to see them happen! *(Have each one lay their head down and rest for five minutes)*.

Something to try: Spray your pillow with some lavender scent and drift off to sleep...it's very relaxing...

Resting our legs, our minds, our energy and our whole bodies is a very good thing. Resting in God's presence brings peace.

Riding on Coattails

This story demonstrates the need to stand on your own two feet.

Preparation: You will need a big blanket or sheet for the character of Mr. Pomp. This will be his robe, or coat of feathers. Pin a red piece of construction paper on the chest of the character that plays Ross. You will need a large area for a pretend bird bath, either a blue sheet crumpled up, or a large tub off to the side of the room (You could just create a round circular area with rope or whatever you have). Finally, you will need three gummy worms.

How to implement this study: Assign the characters of Mr. Pomp, Ross, Fasto and a narrator. Mr. Pomp is a very proud bird that others try to imitate. Ross is a robin red-breast who is a bird that just copies and follows along. Fasto is a small finch, but he's very smart and full of insight.

"Riding on Coattails", what does that mean? It means to use your connection with someone successful to achieve success yourself. Did you know some Christians try to live their Christian life this way? Some kids do this and keep doing it when they become an adult. Their parents may be Christians, so they think if they just go to church and follow the pattern of their parents, they will grow up to be Christians. Other kids idolize a particular person and try to copy their dress, their walk, their success, etc. and spend their whole life trying to copy someone, and never learn to be who God made them to be.

The Bible says there is only one way to be a Christian and that is through a "personal" relationship with Jesus, not through someone else's relationship with him. The Bible also says we are to pattern ourselves after Jesus, not after anyone else here on this earth.

Read Ephesians 5:1. The only person we are to imitate is God. After all, we were made in his image. **_Heb. 6:12_** says to imitate others who are full of faith. **_John 3:16_** is a verse we should all know. It takes a personal faith in Jesus, not a belief in another's person's faith.

Read the following story. Make sure Mr. Pomp's "robe" drags the ground behind him. (Have the "actors" perform the activities mentioned, or help them out by reading the instructions in the parentheses.)

There were two little birds who absolutely adored Mr. Pomp. Mr. Pomp had a long coat of feathers that brushed lightly against the ground behind him. (*Mr. Pomp strolls in front of everyone.*) He also was the most beautifully colored bird in the world. Everyone wanted to be just like him. He walked so proudly with his head held high, and any young bird would jump at the chance to walk in his shadow. Mr. Pomp would invite certain birds to train with him in the art of strutting, cocking of the head, staring down an enemy, graceful takeoffs, endurance for long flights, proper bird bath splashing and of course in looking well groomed and attractive.

Ross, a red-breasted robin, was a young bird who had been invited to train with Mr. Pomp. (*Ross smiles and pushes out his red chest.*) Fasto, a small finch, had also been invited to train. (*Fasto smiles and bows humbly.*)

Their parents were so proud that their babies were chosen to ride on Mr. Pomp's coattails that they could hardly contain their enthusiasm. "Oh yes, did you hear my young Ross is going to train with Mr. Pomp!?" stated Ross' proud papa across the branches to the other parents. Fasto's papa was excited too, but cautious. He encouraged Fasto in private, **"Son, learn well. However, you know where your real strength comes from, and always look to Him for guidance."** Fasto's papa was referring to the creator of the universe, the one who fed them and cared for them daily.

Ross and Fasto arrived on training day and immediately hopped on the feathers of Mr. Pomp. *(Ross and Fasto step onto the tails of the "robe".)* "Show us how fast you can fly!" screeched Ross. Mr. Pomp cocked his head and spoke, "Lesson #1 will be the proper way to strut." As the two young birds sat on the feathers of Mr. Pomp, Mr. Pomp began to strut across the lawn with his head held high. *(Mr. Pomp struts, dragging the birds with him.)*

"Now you two hop off and try." Ross hopped off and then jumped right back on the tail of Mr. Pomp. "I want to be seen with you," he cried. Fasto, however, tried to strut but it just didn't feel natural. He decided to just walk at his own pace, much to the dismay of Mr. Pomp and Ross. *(Ross keeps hopping on and off of the tail, and Fasto walks along, periodically skipping.)*

Mr. Pomp began to cock his head from side to side, "You must look all around you to see which way your enemy might approach or when there is an opportunity for food," he stated to the young birds. Ross began to look from side to side with squinted eyes, looking for trouble. Fasto too looked from side to side, but he was looking at other birds around him and how nice they looked, or how some looked tired and weary. He wanted to remember to come back later and help them. *(Both birds dart their eyes from side to side, Ross with a mean look and Fato with a pleasant look.)*

Just then a worm was spotted slithering in front of Mr. Pomp. *(Someone tosses out the worm in front of Mr. Pomp.)* He bent over quickly, snatching the worm in his mouth, not sharing one piece with his young trainees. Ross saw this and thought how cool it was that Mr. Pomp got that worm so quickly, so he hopped off and grabbed one himself *(Toss a worm to Ross)* and hopped right back on the back of Mr. Pomp. "You're getting heavy," grumbled Mr. Pomp. "Get off and walk by yourself." Of course, Ross didn't move. Fasto had seen a worm and observed the snatch, and he too was satisfied with a tasty worm. *(Toss a worm to Fasto.)* He kept part of it in his beak to share with his little brother when he got back home that evening.

"It's time to learn the takeoff," Mr. Pomp stated as he shook Ross from his feathers. Mr. Pomp showed the young birds how to flap their wings to get momentum going, prior to rising in the wind. Ross was too full from the huge worm he had eaten, and he just sat and watched. (*Ross sits on the floor.*)

Fasto flapped and fluttered, faltering at first, but gaining strength as he continued. "Good, little one," stated Mr. Pomp. "You are very small, but you will be very strong," he stated. *(Fasto flaps and flaps.*) Ross just sneered as they finished the lesson and hopped on the back of Mr. Pomp once again, hoping the bird that just flew by would notice who he was with. (*Ross hops on Mr. Pomp and looks up, pushing out his red chest.)*

"Endurance is the key" stated Mr. Pomp. "When you fly south for the winter, it's a long journey and your wings must be strong, clean and full of feathers. Practice flying. Fly everywhere and build up your strength." Mr. Pomp began to fly low to the ground, showing the birds how to swoop, dive and spin in the air. (*Mr. Pomp performs these moves.*) Fasto was learning and enjoying every minute of it. It was tiring for sure, but he loved it. Ross was still hanging for dear life on the feathers of Mr. Pomp, even though Mr. Pomp had warned him that he would have to let go soon.

Ross was too busy worrying about how he looked, as each time Mr. Pomp swooped, Ross would smile and wave at the other birds, shouting, "Don't you wish you could be me?" Fasto smiled at the other birds too, but he was calling to each one to come join him in the flight. (*Ross tries to stay on the back of Mr. Pomp while he flies, and Fasto practices by himself.)*

It was nearing the end of their lesson, and Mr. Pomp landed in the middle of a huge bird bath in a beautiful garden. *(Mr. Pomp drops his robe and steps into the tub of water.)* Ross slid off for a moment to enjoy the water but stayed right next to Mr. Pomp. Once he almost drowned because Mr. Pomp splashed too much. (*Have Mr. Pomp splash furiously, while Ross covers his face.*) Fasto was on the edge, scooping water in his beak, keeping the lookout for predators above. Mr. Pomp showed each bird how to groom themselves, how to bathe and how to enjoy themselves in the cool water after a long hard day of flight. Fasto learned well and felt ready to conquer the sky. (*Fasto steps inside the bath and relaxes.*) Ross just played in the splashes of Mr. Pomp and didn't bother to straighten his feathers which had become rumpled in the high winds.

Finally, it was time to go home, back to their families. (*Each bird dries, and Mr. Pomp puts his robe back on.*) Fasto had learned well and he had gained strength and knowledge, so he immediately took off and flew home. *(Fasto flies away and sits down.)* Ross looked around for Mr. Pomp so he could hop on his back and fly home. Oh no! Mr. Pomp was gone! *(Ross looks scared.)* Ross hopped to the ground, as it was getting dark. He strutted and cocked his head as he'd seen Mr. Pomp do, but the night was falling and he couldn't see. (*Turn off the lights and have Mr. Pomp sit down.*) Ross tried to flap his wings and fly, but he hadn't cleaned them or straightened his feathers and he just couldn't get off the ground. "Oh, why didn't I learn today? Why did I ride on Mr. Pomp's back the whole day? What was it he trying to show me?"

Mr. Pomp was gone, as he needed his sleep to prepare for the next day's training classes. Ross was too weak to fly home and he was left in the dark, a prey for his enemies to find. Wait! He heard a small voice, "Ross, I'll show you what to do." (*Fasto kneels beside Ross.*) Fasto had returned, because he knew Ross hadn't been paying attention and that Ross had not practiced anything he had been taught that day. Fasto gave Ross a quick lesson, and they both took flight. First Ross cleaned himself in the water, while Fasto kept his head cocked nearby. (*Fasto helps Ross prepare for flight.*) After they finally took flight, they had to stop several times on the way back to their nests, because Ross had very little strength.

At last, Ross and Fasto were back at home in the nests with their parents and families, but only for a visit. (*Both birds sit down.*) Both had learned a lot that day. Training is important. Riding a coattail is not. It's great to be taught and to learn, but one must practice what they are taught and go out and try what they have learned. This will build confidence, endurance and trust. Both birds looked up to their heavenly father and gave thanks that night for the day's activities. Fasto thanked God for his new friend Ross and for the awesome training he had received. (*Fasto flaps his wing and waves at Ross.*) Ross gave thanks for the mercy of his new friend who helped him out, even though he had been silly and thought he could just ride along on the tails of Mr. Pomp. (*Ross smiles back at Fasto.*) He would never again just listen to wise words, but he would try them out himself and become strong.

Both birds drifted off to sleep dreaming of the flights they would be taking together tomorrow to new adventures and new places…

Let's see what we can learn from this story:

1. What was the main difference between Ross and Fasto?
2. Since Ross mostly rode on the back of Mr. Pomp, instead of learning to walk and do things on his own, what happened when it came time for him to fly?
3. What is the main lesson you learned from this story?

When you are a child, you look around and imitate others around you. Make sure those you imitate are Godly people. As you grow, make sure the one you imitate is Jesus and his actions, because he is the source of every good thing and he is the only perfect one who will never fail. Just riding along, copying others and following the crowd, will not make you strong and give you wings to "fly". Learning from the Master and following him will give you wings to "soar".

These shoes are made for walking...

This study will demonstrate how Jesus orders our steps, and how it is most important to wear the right "shoes" when we are "walking" on our journey with Him.

Preparation: Round up the different kinds of shoes listed below, gathering them from all the closets in the house. Line them up in a row, ready for demonstration and modeling.

How to implement this study: As you go over each kind of shoe, let each person get up and model the shoe you are discussing.

Proverbs 20:24 "A man's steps are directed by the Lord."

I Peter 2:21 "To this you were called, because Christ suffered for you, leaving you an example, that you should follow in his steps."

Model each shoe as indicated:

Sandals These shoes are worn when you want your feet to show! You want your feet to look good, so sometimes the toenails are painted, or at least your nails are clean and manicured, so your feet are "attractive". *Read Isaiah 52:7* We want our feet to be beautiful to the people around us, when we are telling them the good news of Jesus.

Tennis shoes These shoes are worn for comfort and for running or playing hard. They offer good support and protection for hard use. I Corinthians 9:24 Run the race for Jesus, knowing you will obtain the prize.

Boots This type of footwear is worn for warmth and used to cover more of the foot, either for protection or warmth. John 8:12 If we follow Jesus always, we will never walk in darkness (cold) but will always have the light of life (warmth).

Dress shoes (High heels) These are worn for dressy occasions to look nice for someone or for some special place. Isaiah 61:10 Let us "dress up" and celebrate with Jesus, like a bride dresses herself for her bridegroom.

Flip flops These type shoes are strictly worn so your feet can relax and be free! Psalm 119:45 Let us walk in the freedom God has given us through Jesus, freedom from sin.

House shoes These shoes are worn at home when you're sick or just want to lie around and feel comfortable. II Corinthians. 1:3, 4 - God always comforts us when we need it, so we can comfort others in their time of need.

Outgrown (too small) shoes These shoes just plain hurt It's time to throw them out and get new ones! Ephesians 4:22-24 - Put off our old ways and walk in the new ways of the Lord.

Shoes that are too big These shoes look funny, like clown shoes, on our feet. They're fun to play in, but not very good to walk in, because you might trip and fall. Proverbs 4:11, 12 Follow Jesus and his ways, so you won't stumble and fall.

Shoes with patterned soles *REMEMBER*, wherever you walk, you leave a footprint. So be careful of the shoes you wear and of the places you go. II John 6: If we walk in obedience and love, our footprints will last forever!

Simmering Stones

In this study, we will make an altar of worship to God.

Preparation: You will need to gather eight large stones/ rocks. Try to find one particular stone that is white, or color it with white chalk. Then you will need some old newspaper, a marker and some matches. If you have a fireplace available, clean it out so you will have a place to build the altar of stones. If you do not have a fireplace, or want to do this bible study outside, you can build it in the backyard in a safe manner. You will place four stones on the bottom, three on top of those four, and one on the top (white). *ADULTS PRESENT AT ALL TIMES.*

How to implement this study: You will be building an altar of thanksgiving and worship to the Lord, one stone at a time. You will write on each stone a specific offering of thanks. Then the altar will be lit on fire (the newspaper in the middle), smoke going up, to represent how the fire of thanksgiving and worship should continually be burning in our hearts.

Read Genesis 8:18-22. **Noah built an altar to God in worship and thanksgiving for being safe and secure in the ark God told him to build. We too should build an altar from time to time to offer up a sweet fragrance of thanksgiving to God.**

1ˢᵗ stone – *Take a stone and write on it "**covenant**", and* read Deut. 4:13. God made a covenant with Moses and wrote commands/laws on stone for the people to obey, and thus walk in blessings. *Place this as the first stone of your altar and repeat together:*

WE GIVE THANKS FOR THE COVENANT AND COMMANDS GIVEN IN YOUR WORD, OH LORD.

2ⁿᵈ stone – *Take a stone and write on it "victory",* and read I Sam. 17:48-50. David obeyed God and obtained the victory over his biggest enemy, with just a small stone. *Place this as the second stone of your altar and repeat together:*

WE GIVE THANKS OH LORD FOR THE VICTORY THAT IS OURS WHEN WE OBEY AND HAVE FAITH IN YOU.

3ʳᵈ stone – *Write on this stone "salvation"* and read Isaiah 28:16. Jesus is the chief CORNERSTONE; he came to fulfill the promise given in the Old Testament and is the basis for our salvation. *Place this stone as the third one in your altar and repeat:*

THANK YOU JESUS FOR BEING THE FOUNDATION FOR OUR SALVATION.

4ᵗʰ stone – *Write on this stone "healing"* and read Ezekiel 11:19-20. We give him our heart of stone (hard heart) and he gives us a new heart, unbroken, undivided. *Place this as the last of the bottom layer of your altar of thanksgiving and worship and repeat:*

THANK YOU FOR HEALING MY BROKEN HEART.

(Now place a small loose wad of newspaper in the middle before you begin your second layer).

5ᵗʰ stone – *Write on this stone "**forgiveness**"* and read John 8:4-11. Jesus forgave the lady and all her accusers left. *Place this stone as the first one in the second layer of your altar and repeat:*

THANK YOU JESUS FOR FORGIVENESS OF SINS.

6ᵗʰ stone – *Write on this stone "**provision**"* (explain this is all the things we need) and read Matt. 7:9-11. God is our heavenly father and gladly provides for all our needs. *Place this stone as the second one in the second layer of your altar and repeat:*

THANK YOU GOD FOR OUR DAILY BREAD.

7ᵗʰ stone – *Write on this stone "**new covenant**"* and read II Cor. 3:2-3. God has now written his commands on our newly formed heart, no longer on tablets of stone, and his commands are to love him with all our heart and love our neighbor as ourselves. *Place this as the last stone on the second layer of your altar and repeat:*

THANK YOU FOR THE NEW COVENANT YOU HAVE WRITTEN ON OUR HEARTS.

(now place a little more paper before placing the last stone...)

8ᵗʰ stone – *Write on this stone (the white one) "**overcomer**"* and read Revelation 2:17. In Bible times, a white stone was used as an admission to a banquet. We are invited to the big banquet/feast in heaven, to be held when Jesus returns. *Place this last stone at the top of the altar and repeat:*

THANK YOU GOD FOR MAKING US OVERCOMERS AND FOR THE HOPE OF HEAVEN!

Now, light the paper at the bottom and watch the fire consume the paper and smoke begin to rise. In this same way, our praises and thanksgivings rise to the Lord and he is pleased.

A Strong Tower

This study reminds us that the name of the Lord is strong and mighty.

Preparation: You will need some light rubber darts or small spit wads, a blanket or cover, a fan, a big rock, a rubber snake and a big question mark on a page.

How to implement this study: Assign the characters of mom, dad, boy and girl, and a narrator. Have the bible open to Psalm 91, to be read throughout the story. Mix it up for fun, assigning the adults the kids' parts, and the kids the adult parts, if you wish. Set up the props ahead of time, read the story and follow along.

Read Proverbs 18:10

THE NAME OF THE LORD IS A STRONG TOWER; THE RIGHTEOUS RUN TO IT AND THEY ARE SAFE.

There is great power in the name of Jesus and his word. Why? It is because his name equals who he is, his nature and his qualities. His name is synonymous with strength, power, salvation, deliverance, healing and peace. There is awesome power in the name of Jesus to those who know him and call him Lord. Jesus is real. His love is real. His power is real. He is the only thing eternal in your life. He is a strong tower and there is safety in him.

As we study, we are going to see how Jesus is a strong tower for us during the course of one day. If we learn to run to him whenever we are in need, we will find that he is faithful and true to those who love him and obey him.

Early in the morning, as the sun peeks in the window, people everywhere are waking up to start their day. People begin to get ready by eating their breakfast, combing their hair and getting dressed for their jobs, school or play. This particular family knows Jesus as their savior and Lord and they acknowledge him every day before they go their separate ways. They hold hands together and pray this prayer, "Jesus, we love you. Jesus, your name is all we need today. Jesus, we pray for protection and peace as we go our separate ways and return home again tonight. Thank you Jesus for all good things."

Of course, there is evil in the world in which this family lives, because the old enemy of the righteous, satan, still goes around roaring as best he can, trying to scare them all. However, this family knows that satan can only roar, he can't harm them.

As one family member Chris steps out the door to head to school, his thoughts get the best of him. *(Chris begins to walk...)* His mind becomes full of fears: fear of the dog he sees way down the street, fear of being lonely at school, fear of failing his test, fear of losing his lunch money *(Everyone begins to toss the rubber darts or spit wads at his back).*

By the time he got to school, it felt as if darts had been thrown at his back and he was hurting, and he wanted to go home. *(Chris hangs his head down).* He turned around and faced the way he had just come and began to remember these verses: *Read Psalm 91:1-2.* He whispered, *"Lord, I trust in you."* It was if the darts fell off one by one and he felt better. He made it through the day just fine. (*Chris sits down and relaxes.*)

Meanwhile, another family member Dad steps out to go to work. (*Dad pretends he is riding a subway*). He takes the subway to work and it's so noisy and hot. Soon, the dry, hot wind of discouragement began to blow at his back. (*Turn on the fan to high, blowing at Dad's back*). It's going to be another hard day at work, where he hasn't made any sales this month. He begins to be bombarded with thoughts of discouragement of how he will pay the bills, how he will afford to fix the car that needs repair, etc. He begins looking down with a frown, when he recalled the next few verses of *Psalm 91, verses 3-4.* He began thanking the Lord for his faithfulness and began to speak his wonderful name. (*Dad speaks the name of Jesus.*) The discouragement he was feeling was gone, and he felt winds of refreshing. (*He faces the breeze and smiles*).

The youngest family member Kate stayed home and didn't go to school yet. She wasn't quite old enough. (*Kate crosses her legs on the sofa.*) She too had her own set of problems. Every time she went to sleep at night she was terrified of the dark. *(She lies down with a cover over her head, trembling).* She would always see shapes and shadows that kept her awake and fear would grip her like an angry dog. She would lie in bed and worry about what could happen while she slept. She was telling her mom about it, and her mom read to her *Psalm 91: 5-10.* She told her how she didn't have to be afraid, because Jesus would watch over her even during the darkest of nights. She began to learn to call on Jesus, her friend and Lord, to come be with her in the dark. (*Kate calls on Jesus).*

Mom went back to get dressed for the day and she began to get discouraged. It seemed with her husband's sales down, the high prices at the stores these days, having to work nights to make extra money and the never-ending housework, she just never could get caught up or rested. It seemed every day brought new obstacles to overcome and frankly, she was just tired! (*Mom stumbles over a rock on the floor and almost falls down.*) She picked up the Word and read a little further in the same chapter of *Psalm 91, verses 11-12.* She began to give thanks for God's protection and asked him to lift her up and take her by the hand. She called on Jesus and he came to her rescue! (*Mom stands up strong.*)

By evening, all of the family members were home and all of them were tired. They had overcome discouragement throughout the day by individually finding refuge in the Word of God and the name of Jesus, but when they all got together, it seemed irritations started to arise. Dad was mad that a toy was left out in the yard. Mom was irritated with both kids for eating too much junk. And both kids were irritated with each other for no reason at all!!! It was as if a big pest had gotten in the house and started nipping at all of them! *(Throw out the rubber snake).* Ouch! The Bible was still open to *Psalm 91* and as dad walked by he read *verses 13-14.* He decided enough was enough, and he began to call on the name of Jesus. He prayed over his family and spoke kindly to his wife and the kids. Pretty soon, everyone was in a better mood. *(Everyone stomps on the snake.)*

When the night was finally ending and all were going to sleep in their beds, (*Everyone lies down*) questions began to filter into mom's mind. Why is life so hard? Dad began to wonder about things, too. Why do I have to work so much? The kids were too tired to question their day, but they did wonder why mom and dad were so grumpy! (*Pass the question mark around to each person.*) Questions began to multiply, until Mom and Dad both shook their heads and finished reading the end of the chapter in *Psalm*

91, verses 15-16. With the name of Jesus on their lips and thanksgiving in their hearts, they fell fast asleep, with the entire family resting under His wings....

Does this day sound like a typical day in the life of any family? Sure it does. Every day is full of surprises, hardships, good times and bad times, and sometimes just our thoughts can ruin a perfectly good day. However, Jesus is a strong tower that cannot be toppled with the winds that blow against us each day. He is strong and his love endures forever. Run to him for protection and help. Run to him for safety. Run to him and rest.

The name of the Lords is a strong tower; the righteous run to it and they are safe.

Sweet Surprise...

This study allows us to enjoy the sweetness of Christ.

Preparation: Make a pan of brownies and have them ready to eat at the end of the study. (Hide them until you're ready to eat them.) Have the following ingredients in small bowls, set out to view and taste: butter, unsweetened chocolate square, egg, sugar, flour, salt, vanilla extract. If you like, you can use the recipe on the last page, or if you're in a hurry, just make brownies from a boxed mix.

How to implement this study: Have a brownie for each one set aside for the end of the study out of sight. As you go through the study, have each one taste each ingredient alone to see how bad many of them taste by themselves. However, when they are stirred together and cooked, a tasty product results.

Life is full of ingredients: happy moments, sad moments, fun times, hard times, busy days, boring days, answers to prayer, unanswered prayers, etc. Sometimes a wonderful day occurs in our life and we think, wow, *I wish every day could be like this day*. Sometimes you have a really bad day and you think, *I hope I never have another day like this*. But each day you have is a gift from God and each day is an ingredient in your life, until you are fully mature, fully made into the image of God and his likeness in every way.

Baked goods are full of ingredients too. Let's taste each ingredient by itself:

Butter is stored in the refrigerator and is firm and hard. It usually has to be softened before it will blend with the other ingredients. In the baking process, creamed butter and sugar together produces tiny bubbles in the batter that expand during the heat of baking. This makes the finished product tasty and moist. Alone, the butter is just too much to take in large amounts, but baked up in a dessert, we just can't get enough. *(Taste the butter)*.

Sometimes we have hard places in our hearts, where we were disappointed or hurt by a friend. We need to let God melt these hard places and expand our hearts again with his warm love. If we do, our friendships will be warm and inviting. *Read Proverbs 28:14.*

Eggs have a hard shell and have to be cracked open to use them in baking, and sometimes they have to be beaten. When eggs are heated or beaten, they turn mixtures from liquid to a solid state. This binds the ingredients together to help prevent crumbling, and gives structure to the baked product. (*Notice the egg cannot even be tasted because it's in a shell*).

Have you ever felt like you were beaten down? Maybe you played horribly in a game or tried you best on a test and failed. Perhaps you had a day where everything went wrong. We need to allow God to take these days where we feel beaten up and let him turn that day into a learning experience that makes us stronger and builds character. *Read Romans 8:28.*

Unsweetened chocolate squares, if they are wrapped and stored in a cool dry place, can last up to 10 years! This is chocolate that has had no sweeteners added to it whatsoever, it is plain and bitter in its rawest form. This is a pure chocolate and provides the most flavor in baking. It tastes terrible on its own but provides intense chocolate flavor when mixed with other ingredients. (*Taste a bit of the chocolate and notice the face each one makes when they bite into it.*)

Sometimes we have to do a task that is extremely hard and we dread it so much. For example, going to the dentist to have a cavity filled! What about having to clean out your closet – a long, tedious task! These may be tasks we have to do only once in a great while, but nevertheless we hate them. Sometimes, doing the hardest things produces the most "flavor" in our lives, or produces the best results. When that closet is clean, you smile. When your cavity is filled, you can eat again. *Read Colossians 3:23.*

I'm sure you know what **sugar** does – it makes things taste good!! Sugar also works as a tenderizer. However, it would not be good to just sit and eat a bowl of sugar; you just might make yourself sick. Mixed with the other ingredients, in the correct amount, sugar provides a very sweet, tasty dessert. *(Taste the sugar and imagine eating a whole bowl of it!)*

We love sugar coated days, where everything is fun, everything is good, everything is well… We know every day is not like this, though, and if every day were like this, we would be the most selfish, spoiled people around! However, when we do have "sugar coated" days, we need to give thanks and appreciate the goodness of God. *Read II Corinthians 9:15.*

Mixed with the other ingredients, **flour** helps hold the steam in from baking, which makes the cake rise, giving it structure. Flour must be measured in correctly, because too much or too little can result in a cake that is too tough or a cake that falls flat or sinks in the middle. *(Taste the flour – yeck!)*

Anger makes our blood boil and rise, making our face red with rage. We must control our anger and not let it get the best of us, or it will result in a tough look, a mean glare and it will leave us with a sinking feeling in our stomachs. When we get angry, we must be sure and take it to God, ask him what do to with our anger. Never let anger get a "rise" out of you. Let your prayers "rise" to Jesus and let him calm your angry heart. *Read Ephesians 4:26, 27.*

Salt enhances the flavorings that are present in the recipe. In other words, it makes the sweet cookies taste even sweeter. It makes the flavorful chocolate cake taste even more scrumptious. By itself, salt is too strong and has a bite to it, but in a recipe the bite is gone and only the sweet taste is strong. *(Taste the salt, can you taste the bite?)*

We are called the salt of the earth. Salt is necessary, but in small doses. If we come on too strong to those around us, sometimes we can become judgmental and full of pride, and others are turned off. Salt makes the flavor of foods stronger. As salt, we should make the flavor of Christ stronger to those around us. Make Christ inviting to others, but don't "bite" them and make them run the other way. *Read Matthew 5:13.*

Vanilla flavoring is used in a very small quantity and is added near the end of the mixing process, so that it stays strong. Pure vanilla is best to use, as any imitation vanillas can leave a bad aftertaste. It only takes a small amount, but it makes a huge difference in the way a baked good tastes. It sweetens and also sends out an aroma that soothes and invites one to see what's baking! *(Just taste a drop of the vanilla.)*

We need to be filled with the Holy Spirit daily, allowing him to be strong in us and send out a sweet aroma to the world around us. Our relationship with Christ needs to be pure, unspotted by the world, not an imitation or a fake. If we are a fake, those around us will get a bad taste in our presence. If we walk in the pure love of Christ, we will send out an aroma to invite others to come, "Taste and see that the Lord is good!" *Read Proverbs 15:26.*

If you take the above ingredients, beat them, stir them, heat them up and bake them, what do you think you will be eating???? *(Let each one guess.) Serve the dessert and let each one enjoy.* Do not be discouraged when you have a bad day, a bad moment or a bad experience. Each thing in your life is working together with the other ingredients of each day, and God is at work, mixing, sweetening, salting, stirring and even heating things up, so that the finished product will be a sweet surprise!

Basic Brownies

1 cup butter or margarine
4 (1-ounce) squares unsweetened chocolate
4 large eggs
2 cups sugar
2 cups all-purpose flour
1/2 teaspoon salt
1 teaspoon vanilla extract
1 1/2 cups chopped walnuts or pecans (optional)

Microwave butter and chocolate squares in a 1-quart microwave-safe bowl at HIGH 2 minutes or until both are melted, stirring once.

Beat eggs at medium speed with an electric mixer; gradually add sugar, beating well.

Add flour, salt, and vanilla, beating well. Stir in chocolate mixture, and, if desired, chopped walnuts. Pour batter into a lightly greased 13- x 9-inch pan.

Bake at 325° for 40 to 45 minutes. Cool in pan on a wire rack. Spread with frosting, if desired, and cut into squares.

(www.kitchenassistant.com)

Swept under the Rug

We will uncover hidden things in this study.

Preparation: You will need the following items put in individual baggies: a little dirt, some leaves, food crumbs, a couple of coins, a ball of hair (out of a hairbrush) and a few pebbles. You will place these baggies under rugs throughout the house, or all under one rug at different places. Also, find a stain somewhere in the house on the floor, and cover it with a rug. Finally, you will need a garbage can near you, to dispose of the things that need to be swept away.

How to implement this study: To sweep something under the rug is to conceal something in the hopes it won't be discovered by others. Have different ones find the things "swept under" the rugs, one at a time and discuss as indicated below. Each item is something commonly found under rugs in a home, and each one will represent a spiritual lesson to be learned. As you discuss each item, open the baggie and dump the item into the trash, where it belongs (except the money!)

Dirt under the rug represents sin that we try to hide from God and from others. Each day ask God to forgive you of anything you may have tried to hide from him or your parents, and he will "sweep away" all the dirt. *Read Psalm 19:12-14. (open the baggie and dispose of the dirt, stating that you will not keep sins hidden, but you will confess them and be forgiven).*

Leaves under the rug represent things we have brought into our lives from "outside", habits we know aren't nice and need to be left "outside". Sometimes we pick up attitudes of those around us, like picking up leaves on our shoes when we enter the house. Pray that the wind of the Holy Spirit will blow those "leaves" out of our heart. *Read Hebrews 12:1. (open the baggie and dispose of the leaves, stating aloud that you will keep yourself clean and not pick up the bad things around you.)*

Food swept under the rug will represent the Word of God that we have neglected to read and feed to our souls. Reading and meditating on God's Word is just like food to your soul, it needs to be eaten and digested, not left to go to waste. *Read James 1:22-25. (open the baggie and dispose of the crumbs, stating that you will be faithful to read the Word of God and obey it, not letting it go to waste).*

Money under a rug represents our talents. Make sure you don't have hidden talents that you aren't willing to use for God. Money is given to you so that you can bless others with it, just like your talents. *Read Luke 6:38. (open this baggie and put the money aside to give, stating you will be faithful to use your talents to bring glory to God).*

Hair swept under a rug represents the forgotten blessings God has given us. Remember his thoughts towards us outnumber the hairs on our head. When we forget to thank God for his kindnesses towards us, we are sweeping hair under the rug. *Read John 20: 26-29. (open the baggie and dispose of the hair, recalling God's goodness in your life).*

Rocks sometimes get stuck in the bottom of our shoes and fall out, ending up under a rug. These will represent little irritations that we allow to stay hidden. Pray and ask God to help you forgive whatever irritations or grudges you hold in your heart. *Read Proverbs 28:13. (open the baggies and dispose of the rocks, stating you will forgive others who have hurt you).*

<u>Stains are sometimes covered up by rugs</u>. But if the rug is moved, the stain shows. (*lift the rug and expose the stain*). Stains are things in your life that you just can't get rid of by yourself. They're the same old things that keep showing up, like anger, jealousy, complaining, fighting, etc. As a family, talk about any "stains" under your "rug" and ask God to make you brand new. Talk about how some stains are easily removed and others are harder to remove. A stain that is allowed to sit for a long time is especially hard to remove. *Read Ephesians 5:25-27.*
Now that the hidden things are revealed, pray together, opening your hands up toward heaven:

Dear Lord,
Thank you for your blood that washes away our sins
when we confess them to you.
Help us to keep ourselves clean, hungry for your Word,
using all our gifts to bless your name.
May our hearts be full of faith towards you and full of
forgiveness towards others.
Give us clean hands and pure hearts.
Amen.

Taste and See

Through tasting, we will demonstrate the goodness of God.

Preparation: You will need to have the following types of candy: (just one piece of each candy for each person). Lemon heads, a candy-coated peanut (peanut M&Ms or chocolate covered peanuts), mini M&Ms, Milkduds, sweet tarts, junior mints, jelly beans (varied flavors), Altoids and juicy fruit gum.

How to implement this study: As you "taste" each candy, you will talk about what kind of taste or flavor they give, and compare this to our "flavor" we give to the world around us. When each person tastes the candy, have them shut their eyes so they can't see what kind it is, and let them describe the first impression they get when they taste it. In this way, it is like a blind (lost) person tasting (experiencing) God for the first time when they're around a believer (the candy itself represents the Christian).

Read Psalm 34:8 – Taste and see that the Lord is good…
People "taste" the Lord by the flavors we offer them, and if it tastes good, they will ask for more. What kind of flavor are you offering?

Sour, with a bite

(Have each one close their eyes, and place a lemon head in their mouths to taste – tell them to state their first

163

impression of the taste) When people are around you, do they make a face and frown like they're eating something sour? Make sure your countenance (facial expression) is one that is inviting, not disgusting, to the ones who are around you. *(Read Proverbs 16:24)*

Candy-coated, but something else on the inside...

(eat candy-coated nut and state first impression,) When you first meet people, are you friendly and nice, but then once you get to know them, a different side of you begins to show? Make sure when people see the real you, there's not a crazy nut underneath your sweet coating. Be real and yourself around others, and be who God made you to be. *(Read Psalm 100:3)* God made us in his image; we don't have to cover it up with something else.

Unnoticeable, unless you're in a group

(Drop the tiny M&M in each person's mouth) Do you hide among the crowd, trying to make sure no one knows you're a Christian, unless you're at church, where you're surrounded by other Christians? Do not be ashamed to be noticed and to let your light shine, even if you stand alone sometimes. (*Read Romans 1:16*)

A dud, hard to chew

(Remember, keeping eyes closed, let them chew on a Milkdud, noticing how difficult it is to chew and how it sticks to your teeth and can become annoying) Do people find you hard to chew, in other words are you always arguing, causing problems, making it hard for people to digest what you're saying? Make sure you use soft words and make peace, instead of making enemies. (*Read II Tim. 2:23, 24*)

Any flavor at all

(Give each one a different flavor of jelly bean) Are you one "flavor" one day and another "flavor" another day? Can your friends depend on you? Are you consistent in your walk with God? Make sure you walk in the spirit daily, constant in your witness for God. *(Read II John 6)*

Fresh to the taste

(Place a mint in each one's mouth) Are you like a fresh mint to those you talk to? Do they feel cool and refreshed after having been with you? *(Read Prov. 25:13)*

Sweet of heart

(Eat this candy, again with eyes closed) Are you sweet on the outside and the inside? Make sure your heart is pure and honest and loving towards those you are around. *(Read James 3:17, 18)*

Curiously strong

(Place an Altoid on the tongue) Do others see you go through hard times and still stand strong? Do your actions and words make them "curious" about where your strength comes from? *(Read Psalm 73:25, 26)*

Juicy Fruit

(Give each one a piece of gum to chew) Are the fruits of the spirit evident in your life – love, joy, peace, etc.? Make sure that when others "taste" what you have to offer, it is "juicy" and full of life! *(Read Colossians 1:10-14)*.
All of these candies we have tasted have a good taste and are pleasurable to most people, but we saw that each one

also had a quality that is not tasteful to some. Some people don't like nuts, or some people don't like a sour taste, etc.

Pray that God will make us have a pleasant countenance, real inside and out, not ashamed of who we are, consistent in our walk with him, a cool taste to those who are hot and thirsty, pure in motive and love, curiously strong and full of the fruits of the spirit.

That's Absurd!

(Absurd: completely devoid of wisdom or good sense)

This study takes a look at the ridiculous things we sometimes believe.

Preparation: You will need the following items: about five stick pretzels and a red circle drawn on a piece of paper, a city map, a full garbage can, a pair of obviously dirty reading glasses, an empty lunch box, a bowl of fruit and a wallet full of dollar bills.

How to implement this study: Tape the red circle on the chest of one person, hand the map to someone, and continue handing out the items mentioned above to each participant. Have them perform the action listed, as you read the study together.

Have you ever seen something and said "That's ridiculous!" "That's crazy!" "That's just nuts!"? We just might be surprised to realize that there are things all of us do that are absolutely absurd. Doing something absurd is doing something without wisdom or good sense. God says if we ask him for wisdom, he will give it to us.

What if you painted a red bull's eye on your chest and sat in front of people throwing sharp darts? (*Have the person with the red dot on them get up, and the others throw pretzels at him.*) Everyone say together, '**THAT'S ABSURD!**"

Did you know that if you disobey God's word and do things you know are wrong, you are like a sitting target for the darts of your biggest enemy? Wisdom calls for hearing and reading God's word, and it brings protection to those who obey.

What if you were sent on a journey to Europe and someone handed you a map of the city where you live in the U.S.? (*Hand someone your city map, and ask them to find the highway to Germany*). **Everyone say together, "THAT'S ABSURD!"**

Did you know that if you try to get to heaven by "reading" the world and following its paths, you won't get there? There is only one road map to heaven and that is through Jesus Christ. Ask for wisdom from above to direct your walk in life.

What if you were hungry and you had a pantry full of food in your house, but you decided to look through the trash to find something to eat? *(Have a person start looking in the garbage can, until they are too disgusted to keep it up...)* Everyone say together "**THAT'S ABSURD!**"

Did you know that you have a storehouse of food to eat in God's word that will feed your soul and satisfy every desire you have? Oftentimes we eat from the "garbage" that is on television or in the movies. It's just like digging through a trash can to find one piece of stale bread. Don't be absurd, eat from God's word.

Wouldn't it be silly to pick up a pair of glasses that were covered with dirt and try to read a book with them? (*Hand someone the dirty pair of glasses and a book to read*.) **You might be able to pick out a few words, but why not just clean the glasses first???? Everyone say together, 'THAT'S ABSURD!"**

Trying to read and understand God's word when we have sin in our hearts is like reading through dirty glasses. But the solution is simple. Just come to God, repent of your sin and ask him to wipe you clean. Then

you can have clear fellowship with him and see what he's trying to say to you.

(Hand the next person the empty lunchbox and have him open it.) How ridiculous it would be to send a kid off to school with an empty lunchbox! How mean! The child would go to lunch, open up his box and see nothing inside and be so disappointed, and hungry! Everyone say together, "**THAT'S ABSURD!**"

When you read and memorize scripture, it's like packing your lunchbox. When you are hungry later, those scriptures you "packed" in your memory come back to you and bring you comfort and hope. However, if nothing was stored, you will end up with an empty lunchbox, so to speak. Wisdom is making sure your "storehouse" is full.

If you had a bowl of fruit to eat, and someone next to you was in bad need of some fruit or they would die, would you continue to eat all the fruit yourself? *(Have someone start gobbling up the fruit in the bowl).* **Everyone say together, "THAT'S ABSURD!"**

Did you know that when your spiritual belly is full, you have been blessed and you are satisfied, there are still others around you who are very hungry for what you have? Don't keep it all for yourself. Share God's word, share his blessings, share your testimony with those around you. You might be surprised at what might happen!

Finally, even if your wallet is full of dollar bills, it would be totally nuts to try to pay for things like love, happiness, security, hope and salvation. Try going in a store to buy these things. *(Have the one with the wallet pretend to shop, asking for happiness and trying to pay for it.)* Everyone say together, "**THAT'S ABSURD!**"

When you need to feel loved, secure, hopeful, peaceful, happy, etc., don't try to "buy" these things by trying to fit in with your friends, be the most popular kid in school or do whatever everyone else is doing. You can't "buy" these things with money or deeds that you do. They come free for the asking through your relationship with Jesus Christ. Wisdom is choosing Jesus for your source of all good things.

Read Proverbs 2:1-15. If we accept the word of God in our hearts, store it up within us and search for it as hidden treasure, the Lord will gives us wisdom and we won't do things that are "absurd". Wisdom will be our shield and protection, it will help us choose good paths to walk and save us from destruction. **Read Proverbs 4:5-7**.

GET WISDOM.

This one's just right!

A lot can be learned just by finding just the right spot.

Preparation: Try to find one of each of the types of chairs listed below and place them around the room.

How to implement this study: As you study each chair and its purpose, let each person try out the chair.

Read James 2:2-4. Sometimes, just the seat we offer others shows what we think of them. Did you know that even the way you treat people you know sometimes shows judgment or selfishness? What kind of seat are you offering your friends when they come into your life? A seat that is comfy and nice to relax in, or one that is only temporary and uncomfortable?

Remember the story of Goldilocks and the Three Bears? The bears came into Goldilocks' house and tried out each chair. One was too hard, or too small, but finally they found one that was just right! One day we will be with God, given the right to sit with him in a place that is "just right" in his presence (Read Rev. 3:21). This study teaches us to offer the best "seat" to people we meet, so that they will feel at home in our presence, and want to be at home in "His" presence. The kind of seat you offer others may be the very thing that leads them to Christ.

Office chair – this type of chair is used for working. Sometimes we offer friends a "seat" only if they will "work" for us. For example, sometimes we may have a friend just for what they can do for us, like share their expensive "toys". All we want is to use their stuff, but not be their friend.

Stool – this type of seat is the most uncomfortable one to offer. It has no back and is usually used at a bar, for a short stay. In a restaurant, the bar stools are usually for people who are just getting a drink and not eating. This would be friends who we just meet quickly, but because they're different or odd, we have no interest in talking to them or getting to know them.

Stadium seat – If you offered a friend this seat in your house, they'd think you were crazy! However, if you were at a place where the seating choices were very hard and you offered a friend this seat, this would be a great kindness. Make sure to notice friends around you who are having a "hard" time fitting in, and offer them your seat, by listening and getting to know them.

Rocking chair – this chair may be offered to a parent or an older person who may want to rock back and forth to relax or to put a child to sleep. This too is a choice seat in a house, offering comfort and relaxation to the person who sits there. Some friends need to have a place where they can just relax and be themselves and be accepted for who they are. Be that friend to someone today.

Lawn chair – this type of chair is used to enjoy the outdoors and rest awhile. But these chairs are only temporary. If there's a storm, you don't want to be sitting in this chair! Be careful that you don't just have "fair weather" friends, friends that you are nice to, but when hard times come, you leave them sitting out in the "storm".

Dining chair – this type of chair is found seated at a table with good food to eat. It is a good thing to invite friends to eat with you. It indicates you are willing to open up and share what you have with them. However, these chairs don't usually have arms and are usually a little hard. After eating, friends usually want to be invited to sit in the next chair…so they can stay awhile…

Comfy chair or sofa –this type of chair is usually the choice seat in the house, because it is the most comfortable. Once a person gets this chair, they usually don't want to give it up. They can sleep in the chair, sit and visit in the chair or just hang out.
Offering this seat to a friend is letting them know they are welcome in your presence, and you are happy to have them around. *(Read Prov. 11:25). What does this verse mean to you?*

Read Proverbs 21:3. This verse means that God wants us to do right towards others at all times, instead of treating others badly and then trying to make up for it. In other words, treat others with the kindness that you know is right, so you don't have to apologize for being unkind later.

When you live this way, offering others a good seat, giving up your comfort in order to comfort them, then you will be blessed by God.

And God raised us up with Christ and seated us with him in heavenly places in Christ Jesus…Ephesians 2:6.

THOSE WHO STAND
ALONE...

This study opens our eyes to the lonely around us.

Preparation: You will need one can each of the following drinks: Dr. Pepper, A&W root beer, Pepsi, Sprite, Coke, 7-Up and a Dasani water bottle. Provide each person a small bathroom-size cup.

How to implement this study: Copy and cut out the slogans on the last page. Set up the cans of soda on the table in a row. As you go through the study, you will place the slogan for each drink around the can, as you learn about those who stand alone, and how you can bless each one of them. There's a clue in each description for you to be able to tell what slogan goes with each soda.

The drink industry is huge in America. Each drink wants to stand out, be noticed and be the most popular drink in America. To do this, they advertise and use catchy slogans and pictures to make you want that particular drink.

There are several types of people around you that feel just the opposite of these soft drinks. They don't stand out, they stand alone.

They want to be noticed, to be loved and to be cared for, but often they are left out and left alone.

As Christians, sometimes we stand alone in our faith and it's difficult. But we have Jesus who is our strength. As Christians, we need to **help those who stand alone by being encouraging, by praying for them and helping out in any way we can.** *Read Isaiah 35:3-4.*

The handicapped – These people are just like you and I, only their bodies don't function normally. Perhaps they were born this way, or maybe an accident caused them to lose function of part of their body. They sometimes feel misunderstood and lonely. *(Find the slogan for Dr. Pepper and place it in front of the can, then pour each one a sip.) Read Acts 3:6-10.*

As you drink the **Dr. Pepper,** which claims to be the most misunderstood soft drink, think of and pray for anyone you know who is handicapped. They need "Dr. Jesus" to heal them, body and soul, and you can help by noticing them and helping them to not feel misunderstood and lonely.

The poor – There are many people in our city and other cities around the world who don't even have food to eat, or clothes to wear. They live in very poor countries with little opportunity, or perhaps they were just born into poverty. They may dream and hope for some sort of escape, where they can have everything they need and more. They want to feel special and experience all the wonderful sensations of life. *(Find the slogan for A&W root beer and place it in front of the can, then pour each one a sip). Read James 2:1-4.*

As you drink the **Root Beer**, which claims to give you a new sensation, pray for the poor in other countries, and anyone you know who is in need. When you see a need, if you have the ability to help, pray and ask God what he would have you do to meet that need. Keep your hands open to share, when God pours blessings out on your life.

The widows/widowers – There are many women/men who have lost their spouses. They might be young or old. They feel very lonely and especially feel out of place when they are around other couples. Often they feel like no one cares for them, and it's hard for them to socialize. The widows who are older often feel like they have nothing to live for. *(Find the slogan for Pepsi and pour a sip). Read James 1:27.*

As you drink the **Pepsi,** which claims it is for those who think young, pray for any widows that you know. Pray that God will help them find purpose and a reason for living, so that their youth is renewed, and they find their place in society. Pray that they won't feel alone, and make a point to greet them and talk to them when you see them.

The lone Christian – There are many kids who attend church alone, they serve God alone and have no support from their families. They come to church and worship in a crowd, but go home and stand alone. They need our love and support, and they need to feel welcome. They were thirsty for God and drank from the living water, but they did it alone. *(Find the slogan for Sprite and pour a sip)Read I Thess. 5:11.*

As you drink the **Sprite**, which tells you to obey your thirst, ask God to help you be obedient by reaching out to those you know who attend church and serve God all alone. It's not easy when you have no support around you, so make sure you support them and love them every time you see them. When those who are thirsty come to Jesus by themselves, we need to make them feel welcome so they will continue to drink.

The orphan – Orphans are kids who have no real family to call their own. They may be foster children or may live in orphanages. Some may lives on the streets. They stand alone in a big world and need big love. We can volunteer to help, give money and pray for the orphans. They need a life that "tastes good". (*Find the slogan for coke and drink*). *Read Psalm 68:5, 6a.*

As you drink the **coke**, and it tastes so good, pray for the orphans around the world. Pray for homes for them, for families for them and for love and provision for them. If you know of a particular orphanage, sign up to receive their newsletters and respond in any way you can to help them their needs. Pray for the workers of the orphanages, as well.

The chameleon – Chameleons blend into their backgrounds and are hard to see. People who are like that feel alone and unnoticed. They feel like they have nothing about them that makes them special or makes them stand out. Often these are the quiet kids who rarely say anything and often get overlooked. *(Find the slogan for 7-Up and drink).* *Read Psalm 139:17, 18.*

As you drink the **7-Up**, look at the slogan which says it's the "uncola". It makes a claim that it is unlike other drinks and stands out as a taste all its own. Chameleons need to feel like they stand out as well. You can boost their confidence by complimenting them and talking to them, bringing them out of their shell. Pray for anyone you know who blends into the background.

The outcast – In a large group at school or in a neighborhood, there's always a kid that dresses different, looks different, acts different than the norm. They are considered to be outcasts, ones who don't fit in. Often they are judged for being different. Often they feel alone, with no one to call a friend. They are not treated well. *(Find the slogan for Dasani water and drink)*.

As you drink the **Dasani** **water**, because you are told to "treat yourself well – every day", make it a point to notice the outcast. Smile at them, be a friend when no one else will be a friend, and accept them for who they are. Pray for anyone you know who appears to be an outcast in your area where you live or play. *Read Psalm 146:5-10.*

All of these drinks are recognizable, they stand out and they attract attention. Those who stand alone need our attention, recognition and love.

AMERICA'S MOST MISUNDERSTOOD SOFT DRINK

THAT FROSTY MUG SENSATION

FOR THOSE WHO THINK YOUNG

OBEY YOUR THIRST

LIFE TASTES GOOD

THE UNCOLA

TREAT YOURSELF WELL. EVERY DAY.

This study examines tools and how they are used.

Preparation: If you have a tool box, gather the pictured items and place them in the box. If you don't have a tool box, a large bag or box can be used.

How to implement this study: Place the tool box in the center of the table or area where you have bible study. Take out one tool at a time and go over the scripture and use of the tool. Lay them out as you talk about them.

At the end of the study, have each person take a tool from the table that they think they need to use, or one that has been used on them lately. Let them explain, then pray for one another.

Everyone needs tools to fix things and keep things in good operating condition. Jesus is working on us to make us into his image. We need to be reminded from time to time of the things in the tool box and the purpose of each tool.

Take out each tool as you discuss:

Hammer (used to hit nails into wood)
Acts 2:23, 24 – Jesus was nailed to the cross for our sins.

Scissors (cuts things, separates)
Isaiah 51:1-2 We are to remember that we came from God, "cut from the rock".

Tweezers (get out small irritating things)
Matt. 7:3-5 Don't try to pick out small things in others, when you need to remove big things in yourself.

Sandpaper (smoothes rough surfaces)
Isaiah 42:16 – God makes the rough places smooth.

Screwdriver (tightens things that are loose)
James 1:26 We must keep a tight rein on our tongue.

Clippers (trims and clips dead or cumbersome branches)
John 15:1, 2 God makes sure we are "trimmed" properly so we can bear much fruit.

Air pump (keeps balls inflated so they are not flat)
Gen 2:7 It is God who gives us our every breath.

Flashlight (illuminates dark places so you can see)
II Sam. 22:29 – The Lord turns our dark places into light.

Pen (used to write down information)
Psalm 45:1 Our tongue is a pen, used to spread the news and praise of God.

Measuring tape (used to size up things) -
Ephesians 3:17-19 God's love is wide and long and high and deep, immeasurable.

Scraper (used to scrape away old paint) –
Ephesians 4:22-24 We are to put away our old life (sinful) and put on the new life (righteous).

Paintbrush (used to create color and beauty) -
Gen. 9:13 when you look at the colors in the rainbow,
remember God's promises.

Glue (used to stick things together) -
Proverbs 18:24 – Jesus is our friend that sticks close to
us, even closer than a brother.

The Umbrella

This study shows us how we are covered in God's awesome protection.

Preparation: You will need four umbrellas if you have them. If you don't, you can move one from room to room. Place one umbrella open in the bathroom, one open in a room under a very bright light, one open in front of a fan turned on high, and the biggest one open in the kitchen on the floor with a blanket spread, and an inviting snack waiting there under the umbrella. (If the weather is nice and you have an umbrella-covered table, use it for this last place). Finally, place a flashlight for use in the bathroom, and "Go Fish" card game under the umbrella by the fan. (or other card game of your choice.)

How to implement this study: As you move around to the different umbrellas stationed around the house, read the paragraphs below and follow the directions. End the study with your snack and with reading Psalm 121 together again, aloud.

Read this passage of scripture together, aloud:

Psalm 121: *I lift up my eyes to the hills – where does my help come from? My help comes from the Lord, the Maker of Heaven and earth. He will not let your foot slip – he who watches over you will not slumber; Indeed, he who watches over Israel will neither slumber nor sleep. The Lord watches over you – the Lord is your shade at your right hand; the sun will not harm you by day, nor the moon by night. The Lord will keep you from all harm – he will watch over your life; the Lord will watch over your coming and going both now and forevermore.*

An umbrella represents protection. Without an umbrella, when it rains you will get wet. Without an umbrella for shade when it's hot, you will get sunburned. When you are at the beach on a windy day, everything you have will be covered with sand if you don't have an umbrella to block the wind. If the weather is just right, a meal outside under an umbrella-covered table is so inviting.

1ˢᵗ umbrella – (*Enter the dark bathroom, turn on the shower full-force, for sound effect*) Can you hear the "rain"? Sometimes standing in a gentle rain is refreshing. However, in a storm with lightning and heavy rain, you need protection. (*Flicker the lights on and off.*) Even the best of umbrellas doesn't keep us dry if the rain is hard and the wind is blowing. However, when the storms of life come at us hard, such as hard times at school, frustrations with friends, fears and worries, etc., God puts up his umbrella of protection and invites us to come under it with him. He even puts a song in our heart so we can "sing in the rain".

(*Sing "Jesus Loves Me" together, while under the umbrella.*) *(*turn off the shower*)

2ⁿᵈ umbrella – (*Everyone enters the room with the most intense light and all lie on the floor, covering their eyes to shield the light.*) Pretend you are lying on the beach and the light is the hot sun. What would happen if you stayed there exposed to the hot sun for eight hours? You would burn terribly and do irreparable damage to your skin. When life turns up the heat and you feel pressured, tired and thirsty, God offers shade. He says the sun cannot harm you if you rest in his shade. Now pretend the light is the moon. What if you lay outside at night for 8 hours under the moon on a clear night, for example, in the dead of winter? You would freeze to death! God is our protection from any outside force, night or day, and he offers covering for us.

(Raise the umbrella so that the light is shielded from your eyes and give thanks aloud for God's protection from harm.)

3rd umbrella –Umbrellas are also used at the beach to shield from wind, sun and sand. The beach represents relaxation and fun, right? But it's not fun if you get burned or if the wind blows sand in your eyes. (*Move the umbrella from the fan and let the wind represent the wind at the beach.*) Even in times when we are relaxing and having a good time, we need God's protection and covering. (*Place the umbrella so that the wind goes around it, instead of in your face.*) There is evil in the world and sometimes it seems like a big gust of wind of discouragement or trouble will blow the sands of life right up in our face, when we least expect it. God never sleeps, as he's always got his watchful eye over us, even when we're at rest and relaxing. Isn't that comforting to know?

(Turn off the fan and play a hand of "go fish" while everyone lies on their stomach near the umbrella.)

4th umbrella –Finally, umbrellas are often on tables where outside dining is present. If the weather is nice, not too hot, not too cold, these tables look so inviting. Somehow the food tastes better and the meal is more enjoyable when you eat outside. The umbrella covers your food and your heads, so that you can eat in peace without being disturbed by birds over your head or a drop of rain, should it begin to fall. Did you know God always has a table spread for us, where we can eat and drink, covered by his protection, communing with him over a long nice meal? He always has the table set and he always offers protection while you eat, when you are finished eating, wherever you go, right now and forevermore.

(Get under the canopy you have created, either indoors or outdoors, and eat your snack together.)

Read ***Psalm 121*** *together again, out loud.*

THANK YOU GOD FOR YOUR PROTECTION OVER US!

Walking with God

Get ready for a nice stroll together with your heavenly father.

Preparation: Pack the following things in a backpack, or have each person carry one of the items in their own packs: A Bible, a copy of this study, water to drink, arm weights and some fruit roll-ups.

How to implement this study: Find a good walking trail in a park or a good walking route in your neighborhood and figure out a time when you can all take a walk together.

Begin reading and following the directions as you begin your walk:

If you look out your window in the morning, you probably will see someone walking. Some people walk fast, others slowly. Some walk alone, others in a group. Some walk in silence and others walk with headphones on their ears. If you visit a local trail, you probably will see lots of people walking. Why do they do it? It's healthy and it's fun, and it brings great benefits to your body.

Did you know that walking with God is healthy and fun, and brings great benefits to you?

Walking – Micah 6:8 says that it is good to walk with God. (*Take out your Bible and read the verse.*) In walking with Him by your side, you will learn what is good, how to act justly and how to love mercy and how to walk humbly. Walking with God is so beneficial; in fact, it is absolutely necessary to maintain a health spiritual life. (*Stretch your muscles before you walk and then walk about 5 minutes.*)

It's good for your heart – walking gets your blood pumping and makes your heart strong. Walking with Jesus is good for your heart because his blood is flowing through your spiritual veins and pumping to your heart, thus making you strong. Water is necessary when walking, because as you walk you get thirsty. (*Take a drink.*) As you walk alongside Jesus you will begin to be thirsty for more of him, so stop and take a drink often by reading the word, praying and worshiping. (*Walk 5 more minutes*).

It increases strength – Walking increases muscle and gives you strong legs, thus increasing your endurance. If you were to enter a marathon, walking and training would be required. You are in a marathon of life and you need strength and endurance to finish the race. (*Read Isa. 40:31*) - Walking renews your spirit and gives you strength to endure so that you don't become weary and tired. (*Take out your arm weights and pass them around, lifting and lowering your arms.*) Waiting on the Lord, listening to him, lifting and lowering your arms in praise and service to him will renew your strength.

Walking increases flexibility: Get those limbs moving and swinging, so that you have full range of motion. (*Walk 5 minutes, swinging your arms and taking big* *strides.)* Walking with God means obeying his commands and loving others, thus increasing your flexibility and stretching your heart to reach out to others. *(Read II John 6)* – Walk in obedience to his commands, walk in love. *(Take out the fruit string and stretch it, then eat it.)* Stretch yourself as you walk with God. Love someone who is unlovable, give when it hurts, offer time for others instead of yourself, etc. All of these things stretch you spiritually so that you remain flexible for God's work.

It allows you time to notice your surroundings – You can stop and smell flowers, pause to observe a beautiful sunset, look at a butterfly as it takes flight, etc. These small wonders of life are missed when we whiz by our surroundings. Take in God's beauty around you and walk slowly at times, taking in every little miracle around you. *(Stop and observe a flower or a shrub, or a bird, whatever is around you...)*

It reduces traffic – Walking gets you off the road and out of traffic jams. It slows you down. When you slow down, you have time to listen and reflect in order to hear what God is saying. You can reflect on his goodness in your life, you can listen to his heart and pray according to his will. *(Walk single file, slowly and with thought, reflecting on the goodness of God in your life, for about 3 minutes.)*

Walking keeps pollutants out of the air – Walking means one less person is driving and one less person is releasing pollutants into the air from the exhaust of a car. Sometimes we need to walk in order to breathe in a refreshing breath of clean air. *(Read John 8:12)* Walking with God keeps us walking in the light, not in darkness. *(Breathe in and out with deep breaths as you walk for 3 more minutes.)*

It helps to shed those excess pounds - Many people walk to shed excess weight. Excess weight causes all sorts of physical problems that can lead to illness and even death. Walking gets the blood flowing, helps you think more clearly, gets you out of the busyness of life, slows you down so you can hear and look around you, etc. All the excess baggage you carry around with you, like worry, frustration, aggravation, etc. can easily be shed, when you walk with your God. You know why? Because he offered to carry them all for you. *(Lay down the backpack and run in place for a few minutes...break a sweat...)* Ahhh, that feels good to know you're burning calories.

Walking is pleasurable - Shed that extra baggage, and you might even find yourself skipping along, instead of walking...*(As you leisurely walk back home or towards your car, skip a little, smile a little and enjoy the end of your walk).* When you have walked with Jesus, stayed flexible in service to him, built up your strength through praise and service, shed those unwanted attitudes and sins, drank from the living water and dined with him, you will end your race by taking flight with Jesus up to heaven. Isn't that awesome? Take a walk with Jesus every day and let his blood pump up your heart to make you healthy and strong so you can endure the race of life. *(Stretch your muscles once again before you rest....)*

"Oh what a tangled web we weave, when first we practice to deceive..." (sir walter scott)

This study takes a look at the way deception casts its web.

Preparation: You will need a large spool of thread, a broken or cracked CD (you can just pretend one is broken), a phone and a piece of paper with these verses written on it: Acts 5:1-11 and I Peter 2: 21-25.

How to implement this study: This study needs to take place in a bedroom with a TV. Place some shoes and book in a messy fashion by the bed. Place the broken CD sort of hidden in a corner. Crumple the paper with the scriptures on it, and place it under the corner of the bed. You will need three "actors" to speak and act out the story as you read along. *(give them a copy of the lesson so they can speak their parts and perform the actions in the story).*

To deceive someone is to cause them to believe something that is untrue, in order to help your own self not get caught in a lie. It is usually very tricky and not easily noticeable, until the tangled web begins to form...

Dee Ceit woke up one morning yawning, because she had gone to bed so very late. She immediately remembered her mom saying that her room needed to be cleaned, before she could go anywhere today. Dee rolled out of bed onto the floor, right on top of her shoes and books. **"Ouch"** she said, as the corner of her book stuck in her rib. Dee just pushed everything under the bed out of sight. She'd clean it all up later.

"Dee", mom called. "Did you clean up your room?"

"The floor's all clear, mom." Dee called. Well, that was true, wasn't it?

(pull string from the bed to the doorknob and back.)

Dee's brother, whose nickname was Spider, came into the room. Dee yelled at him, **"Where's my CD I loaned you last week?"** Spider knew he had stepped on it and cracked it, but he didn't want Dee to know. *"I put that CD back in your room yesterday"*, he said.

Spider had put the broken CD back in his sister's room yesterday, hoping she would find it and think she had broken it.

(pull thread across the room and attach it to a dresser knob).

Dee decided she would look for it later.
Dee and Spider started watching TV in Dee's room and began arguing over what show to watch. Mom walked by the room and said "Thank you Dee for cleaning your room, it looks nice." Dee had a chance then to tell her mom that she hadn't really cleaned it, but instead she just smiled and kept arguing with her brother.

(stretch the thread around the bed and across the room).

At 11:00 a.m., the phone rang and it was Dee and Spider's friend from church, reminding them to read their scripture verses for Sunday, because if they could answer a question from the story they read, they were going to get a prize.

Mom came and told Dee and Spider to turn off the TV and read their paper from last week's service.

Dee and Spider found the paper under the bed, all crumpled up. They turned to **Acts 5:1-11.** (*have Spider read this passage*). "Wow", said Dee. " **Why did that guy and his wife lie?" *"They're stupid"*,** said Spider, as he flipped the TV back on.

The phone rang again, and this time it was Dee's friend, Sarah. Sarah wanted Dee to come over to her house for the afternoon, but Dee was afraid of the huge dog at Sarah's house. Dee didn't tell Sarah the truth, and instead she said **"I'm going shopping all day with my mom."**

(pull string in loops around the room).

After she hung up, Spider said, *"Why didn't you just tell her the truth?"*

"She would just laugh at me," Dee said. So Dee and Spider kept watching TV, still arguing over which channel to choose.

Spider was getting tired of arguing and fighting with his sister, so he had an idea. *"Hey Dee, I think I hear the ice cream truck driving down the street. Go get some money from mom and get us an ice cream."* Dee jumped up and ran downstairs. She was gone about a 15 minutes, just enough time for Spider to finish the program he wanted to watch. He just wanted Dee to leave the room.

(pull the string back and forth across the room attaching it to everything.)

Dee finally returned empty-handed and stepped into the room, stepping over all the strings of deceit that were not visible at first. She didn't see them, but she felt them touching her leg and they felt funny. **"You must have heard something else"**, she said. **"There was no ice cream truck."**

Spider got up, now that his program was over, and began to walk towards the door. He too "felt" the strings of deceit and began to try to step over them. *(have the kids get up and twist into the web).*

Then they both collided and fell over, into the web of deceit they had laid for themselves that morning.

Dee rolled over and looked under her bed and saw the mess she had left. Spider saw the CD out of the corner of his eye that he had carefully placed in Dee's room yesterday.

The strings were so annoying and felt horrible as both kids began to try and get the strings off of them. They actually had to break them and gather them and put them in the trash. It was a messy task.

The story they had read in the Bible earlier began to take on a new meaning to them. Lying is wrong, even if it is sort of the truth.
Dee picked up the crumpled paper they had read earlier and saw that there was one more scripture they had not yet read. (*have Dee Read I Pet. 2:21-25).*

Immediately, Dee began to clean out from under her bed and put her things away. Spider found the broken CD and told his sister the truth. They had gathered up and thrown away about half of the threads they had twisted up across their room. *"What a mess we've made,"* said Spider.

Dee called Sarah back on the phone and asked if perhaps Sarah could come over to Dee's house. Dee admitted she was a bit afraid of Sarah's dog, and Sarah nicely said she could put the dog outside while they played inside. **"Wow"**, said Dee, voicing her thoughts. **"Sarah was really nice."**

Finally, Spider asked Dee to forgive him for lying to her about the ice cream truck. At first Dee was about to be really angry, but she remembered that Spider had asked her nicely at first if he could watch his program, and she had yanked the remote from his hand and said, **"No, this is MY room and MY television**." She easily forgave him. *(pick up and throw away the last bits of string).*

After all was said and done, the room was clean, for real this time. Dee told Mom, **"I'm really sorry for lying."** There were no more funny feelings in Dee and Spider, just good feelings. They both read their scriptures again and prayed together, and asked for forgiveness for their deception. And they gave a big THANKS to God for his love and mercy. *"Here Dee, you pick the channel"*, Spider said, handing Dee the remote.

Deceit is sin, and deceit is lying. Sometimes we deceive in order to get by with something or to protect ourselves from embarrassment. Pray that God will show you areas in your heart where you have deceit, and ask him to forgive you and make things right...

What about him? What about her? Why me?

This study gets the focus off of worrying about others are doing or not doing.

Preparation: You will need a fork and spoon, a book and a bookmark, candle and a match, a hairbrush, pitcher of water and an empty glass, and paper napkin and a cloth napkin. Lay these out in pairs on the table (except the hairbrush).

How to implement this study: As you read along, have someone act out each story as they read it aloud.

Have you ever felt like you weren't treated fairly?

You are asked to get up and help in the kitchen, while your brother sits on the sofa watching TV. "What about him? Why doesn't he have to help?" you ask. You are playing on a team and sprain your ankle really bad and have to sit out for weeks. You ask, "Why me?" You struggle with a test and finally make a B, only to find out the girl next to you made an A. "What about her? Why does she always get a better grade than me?" you wonder.

We humans tend to compare ourselves with others way too much. And it seems we always find someone "better" than us to compare to, not the other way around. For example, what about the kid who has no feet, or the girl who can't read, or the guy playing basketball from a wheelchair? Have you ever wondered why you are so blessed? The disciples were arguing among themselves about who was the greatest.
Read Mark 9:33-37.
Now read the following short stories:

Fork and spoon:

The fork sat by the plate and wondered when in the world the person eating was going to pick him up. He had been using his spoon for 30 minutes now, eating his soup ever so slowly. Finally, the waitress came and took the soup bowl. But wait, the human kept the spoon! When the next plate was served, the human picked up the spoon again and began eating his mashed potatoes. "Who does she think she is, so nice and smooth, perfectly concave and shiny?" thought the fork. "I am clean and ready to be used, what is so special about that spoon?"

Isn't that story silly? A fork and spoon are both useful tools for eating. One is not better than the other, they are just different. **We are all useful in God's kingdom**.

Book and bookmark:

The bookmark was so nicely decorated and small, being placed on page 25, holding the place for the reader. The book was lengthy and interesting, and couldn't wait to be read. Oh, wait! Here comes the reader! The reader picked up the book and threw the bookmark aside. "Ouch!" said the bookmark, "That hurt." The reader read for an hour it seemed, turning page after page in the book. Then the reader did the unthinkable and folded down the page in the book, to mark his place. "Well, that does it!" declared the bookmark. "Being tossed aside is one thing, but being replaced by a folded page???"

The bookmark represents those of us who feel like no one notices us and we always get pushed aside or left behind. Maybe we don't get picked for a team, or we never get called on when we raise our hand to answer. **In God's kingdom, no one is overlooked.**

Candle and match:

A candle and match lay side by side on the table. "Come on", thought the candle. "Somebody come by and strike the match so I can light up this dark room." The match too was tired of just laying there. "Come on", thought the match. "Somebody come strike me and let me burn, and show what I can do!" Finally, the lady of the house did come by and strike the match. He burned immediately and lit up the room. However, she used him to light the candle and then blew him out!

Have you ever felt like you done all the work and someone else received all the recognition? Maybe you worked on a project with some friends at school and you did most of the work. But when it was shown to the class, your friend took all the credit, bragging about what all they did! **Nothing goes unnoticed in God's kingdom.**

Hair and hairbrush:

One morning, a girl got up and looked in the mirror. Yikes, she almost scared herself. She immediately began brushing her hair. The hair said to the brush, "Ouch, you're hurting me and pulling too hard!" The brush replied, "This is my purpose, to straighten you out! You're a mess!" The girl kept brushing and the hair kept pulling. Finally, the girl smiled at her reflection and left the room. The hair yelled back to the brush, "Thanks, I needed that!"

Sometimes we get disciplined because we need it. It's not pleasant for the moment, but when we are "in a mess" it sometimes takes the "brush" of God's word to straighten us out. **In God's kingdom, he disciplines those he loves.**

The pitcher and the glass:

An empty glass sat on the counter right next to a pitcher full of water. "Come on already, fill me up!" thought the glass. "What are you waiting for? Quit just sitting there!" The glass was clean and spotless, just waiting to be filled and used. The pitcher was full to the brim with fresh cool water, just waiting to be poured. Finally, a man entered the room and poured a tall glass of water and drank it until it was empty again. "Ahhhh" said the glass, "It feels so good to be used by a thirsty man!" The glass felt so happy that he had been used for the purpose for which he was created.

In God's kingdom, we all have a place and a use. Keep yourself clean and spotless, stay next to the source of water, Jesus, and he will use you greatly to bless others. In being a blessing to others, you too will be blessed!

The paper napkin and the cloth napkin:

The paper napkins and the cloth napkins lay in the same drawer. Both were depressed one day. The paper napkin said, "We get used all the time and then people just throw us away!" The cloth napkin replied, "Well be thankful you get used. We only get pulled out for special occasions and sometimes only a few times a year!" "Well that's because you're so soft and pretty!" said the paper napkin. "I'm thin, scratchy and hardly anything to look at." The cloth napkin folded over on its side and stared at the paper napkin. "You've got to be kidding! I might be soft, but I get creases in my folds and it hurts when I'm finally pulled out for use!" The napkins continued their conversation, going back and forth about who was the best…

Bickering with ourselves or someone else never does any good. **You are wonderfully made to fulfill God's purpose for you, and you should never compare yourself to someone else**. Be thankful for who you are and the purpose to which you are called.

__Read Luke 9: 46 – 48__. This is the same story again, told by Luke. There are other stories in the Bible like this. Martha was upset with Mary because Mary was just sitting at Jesus' feet instead of helping Martha around the house. (__Luke 10:38-41)__. Jesus told a story of workers who were hired for a certain wage throughout the day, and the ones who worked the longest were upset because the ones hired late in the day got the same pay. (__Matthew 20__). God knows our thoughts. He knows when we compare ourselves to others. __II Corinthians 10:12__ says this is not wise. God knows when we feel like we are unnoticed, and he knows when we need discipline. God knows everything.

We don't need to compare and worry about what everyone else is doing or not doing. We are called to a purpose in life: to love God with all our heart and love our neighbor as ourselves. With this, the Lord will be pleased and will reward those who obey his word.

What kind of friend are you "cracked" up to be?

This study takes a look at friendship.

Preparation: You will need crackers, toppings (cheese spread, olives, peanut butter, chocolate chips, for example), deli meat and cheese, and a hot, fresh loaf of fresh bread and butter. Have them prepared ahead of time on a tray – a few plain crackers, a few crackers with a variety of spreads, and a few tall, double-decker crackers with meat and cheese inside. Then have the loaf of bread fresh and hot, on a plate by itself.

How to implement this study: As you eat each kind of cracker, you will be discussing what type of friend you are "cracked" up to be, by looking at the friends Jesus had and comparing yourself to them.

Greater love has no one than this, that he lay down his life for his friends…(John 15:13)

We all like to have friends, lots of them. But do we like to be a friend to others? What makes a good friend? If we want friends, then we must show ourselves friendly towards others. As we read about Jesus and his "friends" at their last supper before Jesus death, let's see how Jesus' friends treated him.

Jesus disciples

Read Matt. 26:36-45. Jesus was about to face death, and asked his friends to pray with him. Twice he came to them and they had fallen asleep. These friends we will call plain crackers. They aren't all a friend should be "cracked" up to be. They were not supporting Jesus in his time of need.

Eat the plain cracker. A plain cracker is just that – plain, dull and uninteresting, and easily broken under pressure.

Make sure you're a friend that supports others in their time of need, by praying with them for strength and help.

Judas

Read Matt. 26: 1,2, 14, 15, 23, 25 and 27: 1-5. Judas was one of Jesus' followers, and he looked good to others, like he was a loyal disciple. However, Judas was easily swayed to sell out his friendship for money, thus betraying his best friend, and then hanging himself because of the guilt. We'll call this kind of a friend a decorated cracker. This type of friend looks pretty and nice when they're around you, but when a better friend comes along, they change their loyalty. They choose to look like and act like whoever they're around at the time.

Eat a decorated cracker– these crackers are chosen by the toppings and what looks good to you, and you might choose a different cracker each time you eat. Judas was swayed by others around him to change his loyalty and thus betray his best friend, all for money.

Make sure you're a friend who is consistently nice and caring, not just when it's convenient or just when you're with certain people.

Peter

Read Matt. 26:31-35 and 69-75. Peter vowed loyalty to Jesus, but failed under pressure. But Peter wept bitterly and was very sorry for his actions. He did love Jesus and wanted to be restored to friendship with him.

Eat a double-decker cracker – filled with substance inside and out, but just too big to bite and falls apart when you try. Peter had a good heart and good intentions, but fell apart when he was tested. However, Peter did repent and became a strong, trustworthy friend to Jesus.

Make sure if you do fail a friend, by gossiping, betraying or otherwise, that you immediately ask forgiveness and pray that your friendship can be renewed.

Jesus himself

Read Matt. 28: 18-20. Jesus laid down his life on the cross to take on him all the sins of the world, so that we could be free from our sins and have the gift of eternal life. Jesus is a true friend and no one on earth has a greater love and friendship to offer us than his. He died and rose again, giving us authority to go in his name, and promised to be with us forever…

Break the bread and eat it. A fresh, warm loaf of bread is baked, full of aroma and taste, shared easily and very satisfying.

Make sure you thank Jesus for being the best friend of all, and ask him to help you be a true friend to others...

Proverb 17:17 says a friend loves at all times...

What a friend we have in Jesus

What kind of friend are YOU "cracked up" to be?

WHAT KIND OF "VESSEL" ARE YOU?

This study teaches us that different cups/glasses are used for different drinks, all of which are to be poured out. As God's vessels, we too can be "poured out" for others in many different ways.

PREPARATION: Gather the following cups/glasses and put them all on a tray or at the table where you will be studying.

HOW TO IMPLEMENT THIS STUDY: The cups can either be empty or filled. The kids may enjoy tasting a liquid from each one, as you study. At the end of the study, read the note from Jesus and then have the family respond with a note.

Coffee cup – Psalm 17:15 - holds the "energy" drink for the morning, wakes you up. Are you awake and full of energy for God? *(discuss how Jesus satisfies us and gets us going each day)*

Crystal glass – Matt. 23:25, 26– usually very clean and clear, representing purity.

Are you a cleansing drink to those you are around? (*discuss keeping sin out of your life*)

Plastic cup – Matt. 20:22, Luke 22:20 – a cup used by everyday folk, the least lovely among cups.are you used among those around you who aren't loved by others?(*discuss the way Jesus poured out his life for every person, poor or rich*)

To-go cup – Matt. 28: 19,20 – used to take with you. Are you ready to go out to the world and be "poured out"? (*discuss Jesus' command to us to GO and teach others about him*)

Juice glass – I Corinthians 10:16 – used to hold juice, your vitamins for the day, to begin your day with a good start. Are you thankful for each day and your health? (*discuss being thankful for all good things*)

Water glass – Matt. 10:42, Ps. 22:14 – cup of cold water is very refreshing. Are you a cool drink on a hot day to those around you? (*discuss how doing a little thing for someone can mean a lot*)

Soup mug – II Cor. 1:3,4 – holds warm, comforting, nourishing broth.
Are you a comfort to those you are around? (*discuss ways we can comfort others*)

Wine glass – Acts 2:17 – holds the "spirits", used for celebration.
Are you full of the spirit and full of life? (*discuss how being full of Jesus is being full of life*)

Dipping cup – Heb. 13:16 – a sharing cup for those around the table. Are you sharing Jesus with those you meet, by sharing your money, your time and your love? (*discuss how we can be a blessing to others by sharing what we have*)

Measuring cup – Luke 6:38 – used to measure, press down and then pour out.
Are you spilling over with blessings, willing to be "cooked" so you have the best flavor?(*discuss how you can never outgive the Lord*)

This cup is the new covenant in my blood, which is poured out for you. Jesus.
Luke 23:20

Lord I'm a cup full of your forgiveness, mercy and grace, which is poured out for you.
Me

What's bugging you?

This study looks at the little things that eat at us.

Preparation: You will need a potted plant and some tape or glue. Copy and cut out the bugs on the last page and place them around the plant. Tape or glue them under leaves, at the root, on top of a leaf, etc.

How to implement this study: As you read each description below, let someone find a bug on the plant. After you read about the bug and what it does to a plant, remove it. Take inventory of your heart and ask God to remove the bugs that are pests to your spiritual life, by filling in the blanks (aloud) after each description. Pray together for each other.

Aphids - these suck sap from the plant and cause new growth to be stunted or distorted.

What things in your life suck the sap from you? Things we watch on TV or music we listen to that is not uplifting and good, can stunt our growth in the Lord. We can feel sad, depressed and irritable just from what we've been watching or from what we've listening to with our ears.

The bug that sucks on my spiritual life is _____.

Spider mite - these are extremely small and sometimes can only be seen with a magnifying glass. They attack new leaves and buds.

Sometimes when we feel encouraged, new hope and faith emerge in our heart. We feel strong. This is when our enemy, satan, might send a "spider mite" of discouragement through an unkind word spoken by someone, or a condemning thought that he whispers in our ear. When this happens, we need to immediately dismiss it and focus on what God says, not what Satan says, so our faith and hope continues to grow.

The bug that discourages my faith is _____.

Mealybugs - these bugs suck plant sap by inserting long piercing-sucking mouthparts deep into plant tissue and do not cause plants significant injury in low numbers. However, in large numbers mealybugs cause leaf yellowing and/or leaf drop. Mealybugs are difficult to rid plants of because they hide under the leaves or in the folds of the leaves. Plants infested with mealybugs do not always show obvious signs until it's too late and the damage has been done. The best way to control these pests is to check for them often, so that they don't multiply and cause problems. We need to check our hearts daily for bad attitudes, unforgiveness, anger, resentment, etc. Leaving these in our hearts and not giving them to Jesus will only cause the "pest" to multiply. It's a good practice to examine your heart daily, and ask Jesus to forgive you and give to him all of your frustrations, so they don't cause you problems in your life.

The bug that is the hardest for me to control is _____.

Scale insects - these insects have a shell on them that protects them from pesticides. They also secrete a sticky substance that attracts ants and other pests. They are eliminated by touching each insect with a cotton swab of alcohol.

Are there attitudes that you have that attract other bad attitudes to join them? For example, if you are sour and critical of others, people with that same attitude will join up with you and you'll be two sour, critical people. If you continue with this attitude, a whole crowd of sour, critical "friends" may join up with you and pretty soon, no one will realize how unattractive you all are. Take time to think about each word and thought that you have, and make sure they are sweet and kind, not sour and critical.

The bug I have is a bad attitude about _____.

Thrips - these suck leaf juices, tear them up and leave noticeable scars. They are very hard to get rid of and sometimes the plant is so disfigured that it is not even worthy of being displayed or sold. There are some "pests" that we need to avoid from ever even landing in our hearts. These kinds of things are anything to do with the occult or the demonic. Playing with any kind of witchery or magic is very dangerous and these types of activities should never even be considered.

I will not allow this bug into my life and heart (sign your name here) _____.
(if necessary here, think of any influence in this area and ask God to remove it from your heart and mind).

Slugs - A single *slug* can turn a perfect plant into Swiss cheese over night and return to the safety of his hideaway, leaving you to wonder what happened...... As slugs wander about, doing their evil little slug deeds, they leave behind them a trail of slime which invites every other slug to follow to the grand feast. These pests cannot be left alone for even a minute. These type pests are the kind that light on our tongue and cause us to say mean, hurtful things. Hurtful words are immediately damaging and often cause fights and hurt feelings that are irreparable. Hurtful words invite more hurtful words from the one being hurt, and grudges and hatred develop between two people who were once friends.

I'm sorry for the hurtful bugs I've let out (spoken) against _____ .

Mold - this is a type of fungus or mildew. Mold thrives in high humidity, darkness and stagnant air. The best prevention is to provide a good environment for the plant to grow. We can develop "mold" in our lives when we just sit around and let our spiritual environment deteriorate. The best prevention is reading our bible, worshiping daily and spending time talking with God. I need to __ _____ (choose one - worship, read the word, pray) more so that spiritual mold won't have a place in my heart.

Soil insects - these are noticed when brought to the surface during watering. A good drenching with insecticidal soap usually fixes this problem.

A good watering of the word and the Holy Spirit will bring to the surface any little bugs that are crawling around in our hearts. This is the best way to rid yourself of unwanted pests in your life!

Here's a list of how to keep a house plant free of pests:

- Always use clean pots and planters when repotting

- Always use sterile potting soil. Using garden soil can have disastrous effects.

- Promptly remove dead flowers or leaves.

- Give your plant a bath now and then with a soft cloth and a little soapy lukewarm water.

- Examine your plants now and then; don't wait for them to start looking sad. Use a magnifying glass to look for mites

- Proper feeding, care and fresh air make a healthy plant which is more resistant to insect problems.

Read Isaiah 61:3b Did you know that you are a planting of the Lord to be displayed for his glory?
Read Psalm 1:1-3
These verses give spiritual advice on how to keep your spiritual life free of pests:

- Don't hang out with, listen to or follow the wicked (those who do not follow God).
- Don't live with sin in your life.
- Don't be a mocker (A mocker "imitates" or makes fun of something. God doesn't want us to just "imitate" his word, but let it change us and make us real followers of Him.)
- Delight yourself in God's word (worship, fellowship with other believers, etc.)
- Mediate on God's word at all times and hide it in your heart.

Seasonal Bible Studies:

The following pages are devotionals that can be used for different holidays/events throughout the year.

The New Year:

Remembering

This study recalls the faithfulness of God in our lives.

Preparation: You will need 12 votive candles, or tealights, lined up in a row on the coffee table, as you all sit on the sofa and recall God's faithfulness. You will also need wafers and juice for communion. When you begin this study, make sure there are exactly 12 lights on in the house (any kind of lights – ceiling, lamps, nightlights, etc…)

How to implement this study: Let everyone participate and remember as you read along. As you remember each month, you will have someone turn off a light in the house to signify that the past is gone. Someone else will light a votive or tealight to signify God's faithfulness then, and in the coming months ahead.

Remembering God's faithfulness to you and yours is something you need to do often. Recalling specific times in your life where God was faithful is a very good thing, because it reminds you of his presence and builds your faith for the future. We are going to go through all 12 months of the year, recalling to our minds the greatness of our God.
Read Psalm 77:11-12.
January: This is the month of the beginning of the New Year that may be full of surprises. Recall a surprise that

occurred during the past year and enjoy the memory. (*Turn off a light and light a candle*).

February: This is the month of love. Recall people you love who have passed on, or people you love who are still here, and remember a specific thing about them that you love. (*Turn off a light and light a candle*).

March: The winds begin to blow in March as Spring approaches. Spring is when the trees begin to show new leaves and things begin to grow again. Recall an area in your life where you feel you have grown the past year. (*Turn off a light and light a candle.*)

April: Easter is this time of year! We celebrate the death and resurrection of our Lord Jesus Christ! (*Stop and take communion, as you remember the great sacrifice Jesus made for you.*) (*Turn off a light and light a candle.*) *Read I Cor. 11:24-26.*

May: Things are warming up outside, school is almost out, and Memorial Day is at the end of this month. Remember the young men and women who are fighting for our country, away from their homes and family. Pray for their peace and protection. (*Turn off a light and light a candle.*)

June: The weather is getting hot and summer is here. Remember the smells of backyard barbecues? Remember a fun summer activity or trip and recall the great time you had. (*Turn off a light and light a candle.*)

July: Independence Day! Freedom! Remember how Jesus set you free from sin and share what that means to you. (*Turn off a light and light a candle*).

August: It's hot outside and school is about to start up again. This may not be your favorite month of the year at all. Remember something about the past year that wasn't so good, but you made it through and God was with you...so give thanks. (*Turn off a light and light a candle*).

September: Summer exits, as leaves begin to fall. All of nature begins to change colors as the season begins to change. Remember the beauty of fall as you share your favorite color and tell why you love that particular color. (*Turn off a light and light a candle.*)

October: Caramel apples, popcorn, candy corn, fall festivals, crisp autumn air...can you smell it and see it? Close your eyes and remember the sights, smells and tastes that you experience in autumn. Can you remember a specific time when you really experienced God's presence? Share it. (*Turn off a light and light a candle.*)

November: We stop and give thanks during this month while we enjoy the abundance of God in our lives, when we share a big meal together with friends and family. Remember the wonderful gifts and blessings you have received this past year and share a few of them aloud. (*Turn off a light and light a candle*).

December: This is a month we celebrate! We celebrate the birth of Jesus. We celebrate his goodness in our lives by giving gifts to others. We celebrate by listening to wonderful songs of the season. Remember your favorite song of the season and sing a few lines. (*Turn off a light and light a candle*).

Now that you have the 12 candles lit and burning, and all the lights in the house are out, sit and look at the flames. Remember the flaming fire of God's love and his passion for you, how he lights the way in the darkness, how he shines his love into your hearts, how he illuminates your path so that you never walk alone, how his power burns up the lies of the enemy and his quiet presence fills your heart with warmth.

In the quietness and stillness, close your eyes and remember all of these things and ask God to come into your heart in a fresh new way in the coming year, to light the fire in your heart so that you burn brightly for him.

The New Year:

FOUR SEASONS

This study takes us through the changes in life.

Preparation: Set up four rooms in the house to represent the four seasons. **Fall** – Spread a few leaves on the floor and sit on them, have fall-scented candles burning and candy corn for all to enjoy. **Winter** – have a blanket, some hot cider and a fire going, if possible or some Christmas music playing in the background. **Spring** – Place some fresh flowers (or fake) on a table by a vase, turn on a fan for a breeze and turn on all the lights. **Summer** – Have all the lights on, with a picnic blanket spread, sunglasses available, and have the verses from Ecclesiastes (see last page) spread out on the blanket to read.

How to implement this study: Have everyone begin in the "fall" room, moving on to winter, spring and summer. Sit a while in each room, read the scriptures and enjoy the changing seasons.

We have four seasons every year. There are things we enjoy and like about each season. There are things we do not like, as well. Every person is different. Some people only like summer because they're out of school and it's fun to play outside. However, if you live in a climate where it's 100 degrees or more, summer may not be so fun. Some people love the winter because it may snow and they can play or go skiing. However, the workers who shovel the snow may hate winter, because they don't enjoy the snow, as they have to work in it! *Let's look at one week in our lives and see how we have "seasons" that change over the course of even seven days. This study will teach us to enjoy each "season" in our life, knowing that if it's a season we don't enjoy, pretty soon things will change and we will be fine. If we're in a season we love, we know change may come and things may get hard, but the season we love will return again.*

FALL (*Have everyone sit down and enjoy the candy corn in the "fall" room*) –It's crisp outside, leaves are falling, the colors are changing, people are walking. Inside it smells of pumpkin, it feels like change, the bakers are baking and the holidays are coming. Fall might represent a day in your week where it feels like everything's changing and you don't like it. Maybe a friend is moving away. Maybe you had a fight with your parents and you feel sad about it. However, change can be good. In the fall, vibrant colors show and the winds begin to feel cool and crisp. Change is necessary in our lives to make us grow. Share a time when a change in your life came, and how you reacted to it. Are you anticipating any changes in the future?

WINTER (*Move to the "winter" room, cuddle up and sip your drink.*) –It's cold outside, trees are bare, the grass is brown, the skies are gray. You could be lucky and get snow, or you might have snow and consider yourself unlucky! It depends on where you live. In the winter, it's warm inside your home, the fire is glowing, hot drinks are pouring and blankets are covering. If you don't have a home, winter can be bitter and harsh. Winter could represent a day in you week where you feel lonely and blue, and you really don't know why. Maybe you just feel like you have no friends and your skies seem blue. This could be the perfect time for you to sit by the fire read a promise from the Bible, sip a little something warm, relax in the presence by listening to some uplifting music, cover up with a blanket and feel God's arms around you. *(Listen to the music and drink in God's goodness to you. Take time to pray for the homeless in your city, and the homeless in other countries.)*

SPRING – (*Move to the "spring" room and hand each one a flower.*) It's nice to be outside, the wind is cool, the sun is shining, trees are budding and feet feel like skipping. Inside we can open the windows, smell the flowers, feel the breeze and enjoy the brightness of the sun. Even the scent of rain is pleasant and inviting. Spring could represent a day in your week when you have a bounce in your step and everything's coming up roses. The sun is shining and you are smiling. It could even pour down rain, but you wouldn't care, because everything good with you. This is a perfect time to pick some of your "roses" and share them with someone else. When you have a great day and the world is good, smile and share it with a neighbor or a friend. (*As each one places their flower in the vase, have them compliment the person next to them.*)

SUMMER – *(Move to the "summer" room and sit on the blanket.)* It's hot outside, the pool's inviting, hot dogs are grilling and games are playing. Inside it's cool, lemonade is pouring, books are being read and vacations being spent. Summertime means vacation, right? You get a break from school, you might get to travel and experience a new adventure, or you might just soak up some rays by the pool. Summer could represent a day in your week when you feel like resting. You have been busy, you've worked hard, you're a little tired and you need a break. Take a break and drink a cool glass of living water, and see how refreshed you feel! (*Take turns picking up the verses and reading them in order 1-8, and sharing*).

Which season did you like the most???

Next time you have a "bad" day, remember the seasons, how they come and go, all for a reason. Next time you have a "great" day, remember that someone else could be in a different season than you are, so spread a little of that sunshine around to others. Don't let a bad day ruin a whole week. Don't think of just yourself when you have a good day. Every season of our life can be good, when we look forward to change, accept a little rain or thunderstorm, cover up with a blanket when we're cold and share the love when we're happy.

ECCLESIASTES 3:1-8

1. THERE IS A TIME FOR EVERYTHING, AND A SEASON FOR EVERY ACTIVITY UNDER HEAVEN. (*Share your favorite season*).

2. A TIME TO BE BORN AND A TIME TO DIE, A TIME TO PLANT AND A TIME TO UPROOT (*Share how a seed must "die" to bring new life...*)

3. A TIME TO KILL AND A TIME TO HEAL, A TIME TO TEAR DOWN AND A TIME TO BUILD (*Share an experience with building a new house, or watching a building being demolished, or seeing someone healed...*)

4. A TIME TO WEEP AND A TIME TO LAUGH, A TIME TO MOURN AND A TIME TO DANCE (*Share a funny joke. Share a time that made you cry.*)

5. A TIME TO SCATTER STONES AND A TIME TO GATHER THEM, A TIME TO EMBRACE AND A TIME TO REFRAIN. (*Share a time when a friend moved away and how that made you feel.*)

6. A TIME TO SEARCH AND A TIME TO GIVE UP, A TIME TO KEEP AND A TIME TO THROW AWAY. *(Share a keepsake you have that you never want to lose.)*

7. A TIME TO TEAR AND A TIME TO MEND, A TIME TO BE SILENT AND A TIME TO SPEAK. *(Share a time when you should be silent. Share a time when you must speak up.)*

8. A TIME TO LOVE AND A TIME TO HATE, A TIME FOR WAR AND A TIME FOR PEACE. *(Share something about God that you really love, and something about the devil that you really hate...for example, you may love that God is a forgiving God, and you hate that the devil is a liar...)*

Valentine's Day:

A New Heart

This is a study on the love of God poured out in our hearts.

Preparation: Cut out a huge heart from red paper. Write the following words (in pencil) scattered around on the heart, as indicated: DISAPPOINTMENT, DISOBEDIENCE, NOISE, HATE, FEAR, HIDDEN SIN and ANGER. You will also need scissors, a pen, an eraser, white-out and a small piece of masking tape.

How to implement this study: This study shows how that we allow a lot of things to sit in our heart, and sometimes we try ourselves to get rid of these things. But even our best efforts leave marks, and we need to let God give us a clean heart, with no trace of sin. As you go over each word, perform the task indicated, trying to get it out of the heart. You are demonstrating what it's like trying to clean up your heart on your own, without God.

DISAPPOINTMENT – sometimes we get hurt at a friend or someone close to us and we are very disappointed in the way they treated us, or maybe we have a prayer that has not been answered and we are disappointed in God. So we try our best to forgive the person and get rid of our disappointment. (*use an eraser to erase the word* DISAPPOINTMENT *leaving a few visible marks*).

HATE – when we dislike someone so strongly it turns to hate, this makes an ugly mark in our heart. Trying to get rid of it, sometimes we just cover it up. (*put a small piece of masking tape over the word HATE*). Even though it is covered, we know it's still there underneath and may appear at any time.

FEAR – fear takes a huge bite out of our heart and is not a nice thing to have. When we are full of fear, we need an extra dose of faith. FAITH (*use a pen to just change the letters in FEAR to FAITH, leaving some of the fear visible behind the letters you write*). But our faith is sometimes weak, especially when we try to have faith all alone.

HIDDEN SIN – this is the sin that no one else sees but us, like jealousy or envy, or other things we try to hide from others. But these kinds of sins need to be cut out of our heart right away so they don't take root and grow. (*use scissors to cut out HIDDEN SIN*) However, sometimes a big hole is left in our heart that needs to be filled up with something else.

NOISE – This is the part of our heart where we just fill it with other stuff so we don't have to listen to God and what he is saying; it's just noise that blocks out God's voice. We can try to block out the noise ourselves when we sit silently for a while, but very often the noise just reappears. (*use white-out to cover the NOISE*).

ANGER – Anger really darkens the heart. Anger, if left in the heart long enough, can easily turn into hate. Just ignoring it is not good enough; it needs to be completely gone. But sometimes we just think we'll leave it alone and deal with it later. (*use a pen and just put a big X over ANGER*).

DISOBEDIENCE – This is a sin that we often don't realize is there. But anytime we do something that we have been told not to do, it is wrong and it needs to be dealt with. Since this is so often overlooked, we just leave it there. Oops, bad mistake. (leave DISOBEDIENCE alone)

Now look at the heart you have tried to clean up by yourself. (notice it is marked up, has holes in it and looks worn). Talk about how even our best efforts to clean ourselves up are not enough. It takes salvation and faith in Jesus to completely heal a broken, sinful heart.

Read **Ephesians 2:1-8** God is the only one who can save us and erase our sins. We cannot do it by trying to be good or by trying to clean our own hearts. (Talk about how when we do sin, we must be careful to ask forgiveness, and God is very merciful to forgive us and wipe it away, without a trace.) It is all a gift from God.

Have each one take time to be still and pray quietly for a fresh cleansing from God through his mercy, grace and forgiveness.

Valentine's Day:

Left Untreated

In this study, we see that God wants to heal the brokenhearted.

Preparation: You will need the following: band-aids, ace wrap, crutches or a cane, thermometer, Vicks Vaporub and tweezers.

How to implement this study: Assign the characters of narrator, mom and dad, youngest, middle child and oldest daughter. Read along and act out the words in *italics*.

From the time a baby is born, that beautiful baby skin is exposed to the weather and to all types of surroundings, and that body gets bruised and hurt. A baby sometimes scratches himself with his own fingernails and leaves a mark on his face. When he learns to walk, he falls down and gets bruises on his legs and sometimes bumps his head. If he/she plays a sport when they get older, they might strain a muscle or break a bone. What if all of these mishaps occurred and were left untreated, unhealed or just bandaged up and left that way? By the time the child became an adult, he would be covered in bandages, infection and scars.

From the time you become a Christian, your soul encounters wounds, also. As a family, we all encounter hurts and wounds. Sometimes we hurt each other and sometimes the hurt comes from outside the family. Let's look in on one day in the life of a particular family:

Early one morning, the sun came shining through the windows and everyone began their day. The youngest of the family ran into the oldest child's bedroom and jumped right in the middle of the bed. "Wake up" said the youngest. "Go away, stupid!" shouted the oldest, and she pushed the youngest off the bed onto the floor. The oldest called the youngest "stupid" all the time, and it really was hurtful.

The youngest found it hard to hold his head up as he got ready for school because he was so **hurt** by this name-calling every day, every night. In fact, the whole family used words like that all the time. (*Wrap neck brace around youngest to support his neck and head*).

The middle child was a hot-head.

Every time something didn't go his way, he exploded. This morning was no exception. His sister was in the bathroom and he began to bang on the door. "Hurry up!" he screamed. This was his motto, to hurry, hurry, hurry. And when others were slow he was impatient and screamed. Boy was he hot. *(Place the thermometer in his mouth)*.

The sister finally exited the bathroom. Her friend called on the phone to see what she was going to wear to school. The sister bragged about her new outfit she had just gotten and how much it cost and how good it looked, and when she hung up she smiled, knowing it made her friend jealous. (*Place a little Vicks under her nose*). She always went around with her nose in the air, taking deep breaths and smiling at everyone, but inside she was really sick and stopped up with pride.

The middle child began to get dressed as well. As he dressed, he placed several band-aids on his arms and legs, to cover the cuts he constantly had. (*Stick several band-*

aids on him.) He was quite small and everyone at school always made fun of him with cutting remarks. This made him mad and by the end of the day he always felt scratched up and sore. Even though he wore the band-aids to cover the scratches, he could still feel the soreness underneath.

As the kids filed downstairs to grab their lunch and go, mom was sitting at the kitchen table using tweezers to pull out little splinters that she always had in her fingers.

(*Mom pretends to be pulling at a splinter in her finger.*) She was resentful about all the chores she had to do each day, the cleaning, the cooking, the shopping, and her hands were tired. She constantly complained and griped when doing these things, using her hands to bless her family, and this left her hands sore. She never could seem to find that splinter though, so she just got the tweezers out every morning and searched.

Finally, dad showed up. He could barely walk. He had used a cane/crutch for years. He worked hard. For what? Three little brats that screamed and ran through the house. A wife that constantly complained. And he was tired, really tired. He worked hard and gave them all everything they wanted. In fact, he worked night and day, so that they could have the things they begged for, and he was never home. All of this work made tired and caused him to walk with a limp (*Dad walks by with his cane.*)

Take a look at this family. Are they a pitiful sight? The youngest hangs his head in shame, the middle child is full of anger and hurt, the daughter is full of herself and the parents are in bad shape. The mom is constantly irritated and resentful, and the dad is just plain tired and disgusted. (*Have each one get up and demonstrate their hurt, once again.*) Wouldn't it be silly for this family to continue with these hurts until the whole family was unable to function or move? That's what happens when hurts and pain are not treated with proper care and allowed to heal.

The Bible says God came to heal us and make us whole. **Read I Peter 2:23-25.**

How could each of these family members be made whole?

Dad decided that time with his family was important and that it was time to throw down his cane and be an example to them all. He began by repenting of buying and giving every single thing to his family except the most important thing, his time. When the youngest crawled up into his lap, instead of pushing him aside because he had to get to work, he held him close and made him laugh. (*Dad throws down the cane and hugs the youngest and holds him close.*)

Mom lost her tweezers one morning and became so nervous. She realized how miserable she had become and she asked God to forgive her for the resentment she had towards her family. He showed her that everything she did for them was noticed by God and that he was pleased with who she was and he saw every minute she spent giving to her family. This healed Mom's heart and she began serving her family with joy, and no longer had time to spend picking at the irritations under her skin. (*Mom puts away the tweezers.*)

One day at school, the daughter arrived in her new outfit and the girl whom she hated the most showed up in the same outfit! Instead of letting it ruin her day, she began to laugh and it made the other girl laugh, too. They are now best friends. (*The daughter wipes her nose, takes a deep breath and skips around the room.*)

The middle child needed a lot of healing. His hot head and angry heart was affecting his school work and caused most kids to avoid him. One day he just sat on his bed and cried, releasing all the anger and hurt as he prayed. He was tired of being impatient and tired of covering up his scratches every day. One by one, he took off each bandage and asked God to make him well. He now considers himself to be "cool" and he realizes how good he looks, with all of those bandages gone. Once he got the bandages off, his wounds began to heal and scratches were gone, too. *(This child removes the thermometer and the band-aids, rubbing his smooth skin.)*

Finally, the youngest began to notice the change in the other family members and that began to lift his head. *(The other family members remove the neck wrap from the youngest.)* He found himself being invited to join his sister in the morning in bed, so she could hug him and tickle him. He found himself being invited to sit in dad's lap and play a game with mom. Even his brother took time to teach him to tie his shoes, without yelling at him when he messed up. The wholeness of the other family members healed the wounds in the heart of the youngest. He walked with his head held high, not because of pride, but because of the security he felt in a family that was healed and whole.

Jesus suffered for us, and we don't need to hold onto the wounds that are inflicted upon us throughout our lives. Jesus entrusted himself to the one who judges justly. This means when we are wounded or hurt by others, we don't need to hold a grudge or lash out in revenge, because God sees all and judges all. We can rest, completely healed and free, because Jesus is our defense and our Lord and Savior, who bore all our wounds so that we could be healed.

Pray together and ask forgiveness for any wounds or hurts among your family.

Easter:

STRIKE THREE!!!! HE'S OUT!!!

This study talks about Jesus' great sacrifice for us.

Preparation: Prepare hotdogs, an ice bucket, twisted pretzels and drinks. Have a box of Cracker Jacks for each person for dessert, and a white paper napkin.

How to implement this study: You will be eating the all-American lunch with your family while you do this study, and talking about the all-American pastime – baseball. As you prepare and eat your meal together, you will also be reading about the all-World sacrifice fly that Jesus made and comparing that to the game of baseball…

In the game of baseball, three strikes and you're out! Getting called out is not a good thing. It means you didn't get a hit and you didn't get on base. You have to walk in humiliation back the dug out, because you struck out! However…Jesus suffered three "strikes" against him and he got out too! But he got "out" in a very different way…

Read Luke 22:54-62.

Strike One!
DENIAL

The first strike against Jesus was that his follower Peter denied him three times. He implied that he didn't even know Jesus. Have you ever had a friend that you thought was the best friend in the world, and then one day they acted like that didn't even know you???? It hurts! It's sort of like getting cold ice poured down your shirt! Ouch! *(Pour cold ice into your glasses and pour yourself a drink).*

I'm sure Peter wanted to bury his head for treating Jesus so coldly.

Read Luke 22: 63-65

Strike Two!
MOCKERY

The second strike Jesus received was the mockery of the guards. They began to mock and tease him, and even beat him. How insulting this was. Have you ever been teased and insulted because of who you are? Some people in other countries are risking their lives in serving Jesus. Jesus knew who he was and he stood firm, even with this strike against him. *(Fix your hot dogs and grab some pretzels).* Pretzels originate back to 600 AD when they were first formed in the twisted shape to represent arms folded in prayer. Because Jesus had prayed in the garden earlier, he was able to stand firm during all of these strikes against him.

Read Luke 23:13-25.

Strike Three!
CRUCIFIXION

The third strike against Jesus was from the crowd. They wanted him crucified. They preferred to have a murderous prisoner released and chose to crucify our Lord. As they led our Lord away to be crucified, he carried a heavy cross. In chapter 23, verse 34, Jesus stated "FATHER, FORGIVE THEM, FOR THEY DO NOT KNOW WHAT THEY ARE DOING." Thankfully, we have never suffered this strike. Jesus now has suffered three strikes against him. He could have hung his head in humiliation and walked away from fulfilling the reason he came to the earth, but he didn't...

(Open the Cracker Jacks box and search for the "treasure"). A Cracker Jacks box has some insignificant treasure inside, waiting for those who open the box.
Jesus knew that his treasure was in pleasing his father, and that he was sent to earth to die, so that we might become His very significant treasure.

Read Luke 24:1-8

He's out!
RESURRECTION
As mentioned above, in the game of baseball, if you get three strikes you're out! You have to go back to the dugout, feeling very disappointed that you didn't get on base. Jesus suffered three strikes and he was out, too. But he was out of the grave, alive and well, after suffering and dying for our sins.

(As you finish your meal together, take your white paper napkin and wipe your face) Finally, as we clean up with our white paper napkin, this reminds us of two things: Jesus was gone from the tomb and all that was left was a white cloth that was used in his burial. Jesus had indeed risen and was alive! Because of his death and resurrection, our sinful hearts can become clean and white, like the napkin, if we believe and receive Jesus into our heart. *(Give thanks for your sins being washed away, leaving your heart clean and white as snow...)*

Easter:

GO, FIND THE LOST...

This study demonstrates the great love of God that pursues even one that is lost.

Preparation: You will need 100 of a small item (paperclips, pasta, M&Ms, whatever you can find). Place these in a bowl, but take one out and hide it under the bed or under the sofa (remember where you hid it!). You also need 10 coins (9 shiny and one old & tarnished). Place the tarnished one in a separate hidden spot.

How to implement this study: Read through the entire study before beginning. Lay out the 99 and the 9 on a table before everyone.

**** Before the Bible study begins, take something valuable and hide it in a corner somewhere (i.e. place your wedding band in the corner of the tub shelf). Alert the family that you have lost this item and have them help you search until it is found. Rejoice and hug them for helping you find the lost item. You found something of great value that was lost! Now...you can sit down and have the bible study...

Have someone count the small items (there should be 99). Tell them that you had 100 and one is missing. Before going to look for the missing piece, read Luke 15:1-7 and follow along below:

How do we find the lost?

Go after them, don't wait for them to come to you.

Pray and ask God to open your eyes to those around you, those at school, in your neighborhood or those you play with. Seek God and ask him to lead you to those who need him. Obey him when he says "go". Be a friend to the lonely, give to someone in need, smile at those that pass you, offer a prayer to a hurting friend...

Turn on a light.

The light is the word of God. Read it and let it light your path. Take the word with you in your heart so that it guides you every day, in every way, to every place you need to go. (*Read Psalm 119:105*)

Look out from where you are and be willing to try something new.

Once you've decided to go and you have the word of God with you, look around and ask God to reveal to you someone "out there" who needs a friend. Ask God to show you new ways to reach people. Ask God to help you to be bold and unafraid to try something new.

Love one another, as this will attract others to Christ.

The Bible says that others will know we belong to Christ by the love we have for each other. Loving your parents, loving your brothers and sisters, loving your friends and loving your enemies will be like lighting a flame and drawing others to its warmth. (*Read John 13:35*)

Stop now, let each one go after the missing item, by turning on lights, looking in new places and trusting that they will find it. (If hints are needed, give them). Once the item is found, put it back with the 99 and have everyone rejoice, not just the one who found it. Talk about how you had to really look around, move things, use the light, etc. to find the missing piece. (Even though one person will find the missing piece, it took everyone noticing it was missing and everyone searching together, so everyone should rejoice!)

Read Luke 15:8-10. Continue reading below:

Bind up the injured and bring them in.

Many people are hurt and wounded by all sorts of things from their life. Maybe they are missing a parent, maybe they have been abused, maybe they have an illness, etc. The truth is, we don't know the reasons behind the way others act. Sometimes just listening to a friend brings healing to their heart. Sometimes a kind word heals wounded soul. Sometimes a prayer could save a life. *(Read Isaiah 61:1)*

Strengthen the weak and help them stand.

There are many who choose to follow Christ, but perhaps they are the only one in their family who is a believer. They are weak and have no one to support them and encourage them to be strong. We can come alongside them and lift up the weak hands, and strengthen the knees that bend. (*Read Isaiah 35:3,4*).

Carry the lame (not on your shoulders, but bring them to Jesus)

There are many who are just too sick and lame to even walk with Jesus. These might be those who are in juvenile homes, those who are in mental hospitals, those who are high on drugs, etc. They are so ill that they need to be rescued. You can pray and believe and call their name to

Jesus and ask him to carry them in to his presence and set them free…

Stop now and have everyone search for the tarnished coin. When it is found, place it with the shiny coins and rejoice. Remind yourselves how the weak and lame don't feel like they fit in, because they look different. It takes care, love and patience to help them grow and mature into a new shiny coin again.

End the study by praying for the lost and by praying that we will have eyes to see the lost and compassion to bring them to Jesus.

Summer:

ROOTS

This Bible study will teach about good roots and bad roots, shallow roots and deep roots, and how to let the good things grow deep in our hearts.

Preparation: Go outside in the yard (or you could go to a park) and find five different types of plants that can be used: leaves, grass, weeds, flowering plant and a large bush or small tree.

How to implement this study: Have the family go out back around the picnic table or on a blanket. Let the children participate by going to pull each plant as you read about the root system.

Leaves - *(find a few leaves and put them on the table or in the center of the blanket)* – Leaves have no roots at all, they have fallen off the branch. *(blow the leaves)* – When the wind comes, they are blown away because they are not attached to anything. (Eph. 4:14,15) – We don't want to be like the leaves, blowing around. Instead, we want to have roots and grow. (John 15:4) – We must be "connected" to Jesus in order to grow.

The next few things we look at will have roots. Shallow root systems are easily pulled out, but deep ones are very hard to pull. We will talk about being careful about what things we let take "root" in our heart.

Grass - (*pull a few blades of grass, trying to pull from the root*) – Grass has a very shallow root system, very easy to pull. (*show the depth of the root*). Grass is a good thing to have in your yard, but the roots are shallow and the grass must be watered frequently in order to stay alive. (*Colossians 1:10*) – We must grow in our knowledge of God through reading his word and praying to him. This keeps our "spiritual yard" nice and green.

Weeds - (*find two weeds, pull one by the root and break off the other one*) – Weeds may have a flower and look pretty for a time, but they must be pulled. They must be pulled from the root or they will grow back. (*I Tim 6:10, Eph. 4:29-32*) Weeds that grow in our hearts can be anger, hatred, unforgiving spirit, etc.) These must be "pulled" from the root.

Flowers - (*find a flowering plant that has a secure root system and talk about the root system of that flower.*) If you want to cut a flower and enjoy it, do so. Try to find a fragrant one. Do not pull up the flower, because it is a good root that needs to grow. – Flowers are only produced after the plant has taken root and been fed properly. (*II Cor. 2:14, 15*) – We are to let God live in us so that we are a beautiful fragrance to all those around us.

Bushes or trees - (*try to pull up a tree with your hands and see that you cannot do it*) – Trees or bushes have deep roots. Some trees are hundreds of years old and can only be uprooted with a machine. Their roots run deep and if they are near a water source, they are grounded and prosper, with beautiful green leaves for all to enjoy. (*Psalm 1:1-3*) If we let the good roots grow deep in our walk with Jesus, we will be strong and immovable like the trees, full of large branches and fruit for all to enjoy.

At the end of this study, you may want to let each one think of any roots they may have that they need to "pull", and pray for each other. After that is done, pray for each other that the scriptures they read will take root and grow in their hearts.

Summer:

Water

In this study, we enjoy the refreshing aspects of water.

Preparation: You will need a wet cloth, a spray bottle full of water, a sprinkler going, a watering can full of water, glasses of ice water for each person, a plate of sugar cookies, a Frisbee and a large bowl of water. Place the bowl of water outside the day before the lesson. Have each one come in their bathing suit, or in clothes they can get wet. Provide towels. Set up the backyard with all these items spread around, including a chair for each person, prior to the study.

How to implement this study: You need a warm day or evening to have this study. This study teaches about the wonderful properties of water. Follow the instructions below.

Why do we need water?????

Water cleanses us

(*Take the wet cloth and pass it around, washing your hands or face*). The word of God within in us cleanses us and erases all stains. *Read Ephesians 5:25-27*

Water refreshes

(*Spray each one with the water bottle, to cool them off*). When we repent, or turn from our sin, then we are refreshed, made new. *Read Acts 3:19*

Water makes things grow

(Use the watering can and water the plants in the yard). Roots are established when there is an abundance of water. *Read Psalm 1:1-3*

Water quenches our thirst

(Give everyone a glass of water to drink, along with a cookie to eat) Nothing satisfies on a hot day, like a cool drink of water. *Read John 7:37, 38*

Water is soothing

(Have everyone close their eyes and listen to the water from the sprinkler) Just the sound of water gently flowing brings restoration to the soul, or even just the sight of it. This is why many people enjoy vacationing near or surrounded by water. *Read Psalm 23: 1-3*

Water must flow or it becomes stagnant

(Observe the bowl of water that has been there overnight). Springs of water bring satisfy, but stagnant water attracts disease. *Read Isaiah 58:11*

Water recycles

(Observe the sky and the clouds) Water falls, waters the earth, returns again, accomplishing its purpose. *Read Isaiah 55: 10-11*

Water covers wherever it is spread.

(Throw the Frisbee to each other, symbolizing spreading the gospel). The earth will be full of the knowledge of the Lord when his word goes forth. *Read Isaiah 11:9*

Water is a part of all living things……it's eternal

(Have each one pray and give thanks for one of the aspects of water.) Water is a symbol of life everlasting. *Read Rev. 7:17*

Fall/Autumn:

Buying Gold

This study makes us want to search for "gold".

Preparation: This bible study is to be done around a fire: either the fireplace, a campfire or even a fondue pot or candle at the table. ADULT SUPERVISION AT ALL TIMES.   You will be making s'mores together and will need a fireproof wire or hanger for each person, large marshmallows, whole chocolate Hershey bars and graham crackers. Provide water and napkins.

How to implement this study: As you all sit around the fire, you will be learning about "buying gold that's been tried in the fire" and what that means, while you make s'mores together.

READ REVELATION 3:18

We are going to learn what it means to "buy gold" that's been tried in the fire. Gold is a very precious metal to human beings. Having lots of gold jewelry can be a sign of wealth. Winning a gold metal is a sign of great achievement. A person who finds a treasure chest full of gold coins would suddenly have lots of friends. A pot of gold is supposed to be at the end of every rainbow…but have you ever found one? In history, we read about settlers going west to pan for gold, so they could become rich! "Go for the gold" is a term we know to mean to try to achieve the top rank in whatever you're doing. Win the race, be proud, finish before everyone else, be the best….for what? So you'll be famous and wealthy? Fame and wealth don't last forever, but going after God's gold does last forever and ever…and with it are great rewards.

When making s'mores we use a metal wire or rod to place in the fire because it won't burn. (*Give each one their wire*). The wire is strong and secure, and nothing else will do. Jesus is our strength and security and nothing else will do. The first "gold" you need to buy is trust (Read Job 28: 12, 28). This is the "gold" that backs up everything else in your life. Trust in who God is, what he does and how he does it. He knows when to put you in the fire (testing), how long and when to pull you out, all to make you moldable and tastier, not to destroy you.

The next thing you need to make a s'more is two graham crackers. (*Give each one a cracker*). The graham crackers are the top and bottom of the s'more and they hold it together. The first cracker is going to symbolize the next "gold" you need, which is "righteousness". You can't buy this on your own, you need a savior and his name is Jesus. The Bible says he is our righteousness. (Read II Corinthians 9:9).

(*Break the cracker in half so there are two pieces*). The second graham cracker is going to symbolize "a good name". (Read Proverbs 22:1). Honesty, kindness, generosity, etc. are qualities in a person that result in the person having a good name. Righteousness and a good name are the two "gold" bars that we need in our lives. Righteousness comes from knowing Jesus and his forgiveness, and a good name comes from living for Jesus daily, obeying his commands.

One important thing that makes the s'more yummy is a square of chocolate. (Read Psalm 119:127). This "gold" is "loving God's word more than life". We break the chocolate in order to fit the cracker, and the chocolate gets warm when we place the hot marshmallow on it, and it tastes oh so good. God's word tastes good and sometimes it breaks us so we can "fit" into God's plan for our lives, but the result is oh so good. (*Break off a piece of the chocolate bar to fit the cracker*).

The last part of the s'more is the marshmallow. (*Give each one a big marshmallow*). This is going to represent "wisdom", which is the "gold" that we are ask God to give us. Wisdom is the ability to judge what is right, true and lasting. The marshmallow is the ingredient of a s'more that is the final touch, to make your s'more complete. When you ask and receive wisdom from God, it's like the icing on the cake, the whip cream on a sundae, the marshmallow in a s'more. (Read Proverbs 3:13-15).

(Have each one assemble their crackers and chocolate, ready to receive the roasted marshmallow).

Finally, roasting the marshmallow makes is soft and gooey, easily spread on the cracker. (Read Job 23:10). Remember, the wire is our security, Jesus, and we can rest assured that when we are connected to him, any test or trial that comes our way is only for good. He knows exactly how much fire we can take, and he is the one who keeps us from getting burned.
(*Roast the marshmallow and make your s'more*). Testing us through the fire brings forth gold.

(Read Job 42:10) – Job's ability to pray for his enemies brought great blessings upon his life, after all losing it all. *(Eat the s'more)*. As you eat your snack, which represents all the gold you now possess – wisdom, security in Jesus, righteousness, loving God's word and a good name – pray for all those around you are against you or against God. Pray and believe that while you are praying for others, you will bring blessings to your own life.

(Discuss together how buying gold may require testing in our lives and some hard things we have to go through, but the end result is pure everlasting gold)

I counsel you to buy from me gold refined in the fire, so you can become rich: and white clothes to wear, so you can cover your shameful nakedness, and salve to put on your eyes, so you can see.
Revelation 3:18

Halloween:

The Masks we Wear

This study is about hiding behind masks.

Preparation: You will need a large leafy tree branch, a black scarf or piece of material, a stuffed animal or stuffed clown, a bandana and dark glasses, a section of the newspaper, a piece of paper with two cut-outs for eyes, and a large piece of foil.

How to implement this study: This study talks about the different "faces" we put on, and the ways we "hide", so that others can't see who we really are. As you read over each "mask", have someone put it up in front of their face to show how it looks and act out the emotion. (Keep the masks in a bag and pull them out one at a time). Pray that we will take off our masks and let others see who we are in Christ.

Reasons "masks" are worn:

1. To become a character in a play, to become someone we are not - (*use the cut-out paper for a mask*) God loves who he made us to be, we don't' have to "pretend" to be someone else.

Talk about how we look at others that we envy or admire, like stars on TV or popular kids at school, etc., but we should look at Jesus and try to be like him instead. (Psalm 105:4)

2. To hide, when we've done something wrong – *(have someone tie the bandana around their face and put on the dark glasses) –*

Talk about how when we sin or disobey, we try to run and hide so no one will see, but instead we should confess our sin and come to Jesus, and he will forgive. Then we won't need to hide. (Psalm 34:5)

3.   To ignore others around us, pretending we don't hear them or see them - *(have someone pretend they are reading the newspaper, hiding their face behind it)*

Talk about how there's a time for everything, a time to read, and a time to listen. When someone is talking to us or instructing us, like our parents, or a friend, we should put down what we're doing and really listen. (Phil. 2:4)

4.   To protect us from getting hurt – *(have someone wear the knight "foil" mask)* – Helmet and masks are worn in battle to protect from injury.

Talk about how Jesus is our protector, and the word in our heart is our sword, so we can boldly face the "enemy" of our soul, the devil. We don't have to be afraid. (II Thes. 3:3)

5.   To blend in with the crowd around us – (*if you have a potted plant, have someone squat beside it with the branch in front of their face*)

Talk about how becoming part of a crowd is not always a good thing. Be proud to be who God made you to be. (II Cor. 6:17)

6.   To look mean and scare people away – (*place black scarf over head and say "boo"*) –

Discuss how we need to make sure our countenance, the expression on our face, shows the radiance (brightness) of Jesus. (Psalm 34:5 again)

7.   To be silly or amusing - (*use the stuffed animal or clown to hide behind*) – it's okay to be silly sometimes, but not when we're supposed to be listening or working.

Discuss how sometimes we act silly because we're nervous or uncomfortable. God can help us when we're anxious, if we let him. (I Pet. 5:7)

Stuff all the masks back inside the bag and smile, thanking God that you can be just who you are with him, and you do not have to hide behind anything.

Halloween:

Trick or Treat?

This study trains us to detect "tricks" and only receive "treats".

Preparation: You will need the following items set out on a table or tray: two different dark colas in clear glasses, a spoonful of salt and a spoonful of sugar, a fake leaf or flower and a real leaf or flower, a piece of gum in the wrapper and an empty wrapper that looks like it has gum in it, a broken cookie put back together and an unbroken cookie, a fake dollar (like from a monopoly game) and a real dollar, an empty box of cereal and a full one, a spoon of chili powder and one of paprika, a wallet with money and one with no money, two keys that look similar but fit different things (keys that the kids won't recognize) and finally, two phones with different ringer tones.

How to implement this study: The purpose of this study is to teach us how to tell if something is a "trick" or a "treat". Very often in life, we are faced with choices and temptations and we need skills to determine when something is real or not, good or bad, useful or damaging, etc. You will follow along with the directions below.

Trick or Treat? Look at the two glasses of soda. How can you tell which is which? By tasting! The only way you can know the goodness of the Lord is to "**taste and see**" his goodness by getting to know him personally. And if you taste the goodness of the Lord, you won't be tempted to taste the evil things in the world. *(Read I Peter 2:2,3) (Guess the soda, then taste)*

Trick or Treat? Have you ever accidentally put salt in your tea instead of sugar? What an unpleasant surprise!

Upon close examination, you can see the difference between salt and sugar. But from a distance, it may be hard to tell. They also taste very, very different from each other. **Closely examine the word of God** and hide it in your heart, so you won't be deceived by the tricks that come your way. *(Read Acts 17:11) (Guess which is salt and which is sugar; then see if you're right)*

Trick or Treat? How can you tell a fake plant from a real one? Sometimes it's obvious by just looking, or you may have to feel it with your fingers or smell it with your nose. Take time to **study** God's word, **look** into it, **experience** it, smell it, etc. By doing this, you will easily recognize anything counterfeit that comes your way. *(feel the leaves and their differences)*

Trick or Treat? Which piece of gum would you like to have? Do they both look the same? When you pick them up, you will realize one wrapper is empty. They both appeared to be full, but one was not. **Don't always judge things by outward appearances**. Looks can be deceiving. *(Read II Thessalonians 2:3a) (pick the real gum)*

Trick or Treat? Both cookies look good on the plate. But if you start to pick one up, the broken one will be obvious. It wasn't easy to tell it was broken when the cookies were lying on the table, because someone had tried to make it look like the other one. Only God can fix a broken heart. **Don't pretend** that everything's okay when it's broken. Go to Him and let him make you whole. *(Read Psalm 147:3)(guess which cookie is whole, which is not)*

Trick or Treat? How do you tell real dollars from fake ones? Well, in this case it's obvious by just looking. But if you worked at a bank, you'd have to know the feel of a real dollar and **hold it up to the light** to see if it's the real deal. Hold everything you are unsure about up against the light of God's word to see if it's the real thing. Then hold fast to that which is real and discard that which is not. *(Read Psalm 36:9)(pick up the obvious dollar, hold it up to the light)*

Trick or Treat? Which cereal box is empty? You can't tell without picking it up and shaking it. If something is empty it should be refilled or thrown away, not left in the pantry. Nothing is so frustrating as to be hungry, pick up a box of cereal and find it is empty. **Shake it up** and see what's in it, so you can keep it full and running over. *(shake the boxes to see which one's full)*

Trick or Treat? You can smell the difference between these two spices before you ever taste them. And if you choose to taste them, by themselves, you might get quite a bite! **Discern a situation**, "sniff it out", before choosing to participate or be a part of a group or activity. The Holy Spirit will guide you and lead you, so you won't be tricked. *(Read Philippians 1:9,10)(smell or gently taste the spices to see the difference)*

Trick or Treat? If you have a padded wallet in your pocket, that doesn't mean you have lots of money. The only way to tell if a wallet has money inside is to open it! And the money is of no good to you if the wallet is not opened and the money is not spent! This is the way it is with the word of God. **Open your bible, read it, see what it says**. You will find a real treasure when you do. *(Read Colossians 2:3)(open the wallets, look inside)*

Trick or Treat? Lots of keys look similar to one another, but keys only fit certain locks. A similar-looking key will not open a lock unless it was made exactly for that lock. The only way to know if a key works is to try it. Insert it into the lock and turn. Does the door open? The world offers its "keys" to success and fame, and God offers his "keys" to an abundant life in Him. God's keys work, all the time, because he made you and formed you to "fit" a specific purpose and design he has for your life! **Unlock your faith** and see his goodness in your life. *(find out what the keys unlock)*

<u>Trick or Treat?</u> A phone rings, you listen for the sound. Do you recognize it? Is it the cell phone ringing or the house phone? You know the phone by the sound of its ring. God gave you ears to hear, to listen. **Listen to Him** and get to know his voice. Learn to recognize when he is calling and listen to what he says. *(Read Rev. 3:20)(use one phone to call the other, did you recognize the sound?)*

Trick or Treat?
Is it good to eat?
Taste and see.

Trick or treat?
Do you know the sound?
Listen and hear.

Trick or treat?
Does it look good in the light?
Hold it up and see.

Trick or treat?
Is it broken or whole?
Give it to Jesus.

Trick or treat?
Does it fit with the Word?
Unlock your faith and believe.

Trick or treat?
Is it full of life?
Shake it up and see.

Thanksgiving:

Thanks!

In this study, we offer up thanks.

Preparation: Have the family members come prepared to this bible study by bringing at least one each of the following – a song of thanks (one everyone knows, or they can write one themselves), a psalm from the bible (i.e. Psalm 35:18, Psalm 28:7, etc.) giving thanks, a written prayer full of thanksgiving, crackers and juice (for communion) and finally, you bring separate papers with each person's name written at the top and pencil for each person. Hand out these assignments a little while prior to bible study, so each one comes prepared.

How to implement this study: This study is designed to allow us time to reflect on the goodness of God in our lives and to offer up thanksgiving. As you read about how harvest festivals were celebrated in ancient times around the world, stop and reflect on how thankful you are to serve a living God full of goodness and mercy. After reading each description below, give thanks using the items each one has brought to the study.

Efcharisto (Greek – ef-a-rist-<u>o</u>) – The Greeks worshipped many gods, and at their harvest festivals, they would worship the goddess of corn. We worship **one God, our Lord and Savior Jesus Christ**, and we give thanks for his abundance in our lives, providing food, shelter and clothing.

(stop here and allow the person who brought the psalm to read it aloud, then have everyone recite it with them).

Gratias (Latin) – Latin was the original language spoken in Rome. Their festival offered crops and pigs to their god, and they celebrated with music and games. We give thanks by **giving of our blessings to others**, because Jesus said when we give to others, we are giving to him.

(Hand out the papers around to each other, have each one write a thanks to that person. The result will be that each person gets the paper back with their name on it, with a word of thanks from each person in the family).

XIE XIE (Chinese – <u>si</u>-e-<u>si</u>-e) – The Chinese celebrated the birthday of the moon, whenever it was full. They would bake moon cakes and believed the flowers would fall from the moon and whoever saw them would be blessed. We believe that whoever believes on the Lord Jesus Christ will be saved, and **goodness and mercy will follow** them all the days of their lives.

(stop here and sing the song or have the person sing the song they chose to bring).

toda (Hebrew) - They celebrate Sukkoth, which is a feast to celebrate the huts that Moses and the Israelites lived in before they reached the Promised Land. They built small temporary huts out of branches, loosely put together so that light could come in. They would eat their meals in the huts under the evening sky. We know that God dwells in our hearts and all we have to do is **open our heart to let the "light of the world" (Jesus) inside.**

(have the person read or say their prayer of thanksgiving to Jesus)

SHOKRAN (Arabic) – In ancient Egypt, they celebrated their god of the harvest with a festival. When they harvested their corn, they cried and pretended to be very sad in hopes to deceive the spirit they thought lived in

the corn. We don't have to pretend to cry or try to deceive anyone, as we have the **Holy Spirit living in us**. He brings us joy, peace and comfort.

(Read Phillipians 4:4-7, then say a prayer aloud)

Thank You. In the United States, the Pilgrims
celebrated with a feast, giving thanks to God for having endured and overcome the obstacles of the new world. They had plenty of food and had made peace with the Indians, and gave thanks to God for his blessings. We too **celebrate our Lord's goodness** in our lives by having a Thanksgiving feast together with our families.

(Read I. Cor. 11:24-26 and then have communion with your family, using the juice and crackers, giving thanks for Jesus and what he's done for you)

(information on the ancient festivals was gathered from the website http://www.holidays.net/thanksgiving/story.htm)

Thanksgiving:

Got the blues?
Give thanks.

This study allows us to be creative in giving thanks.

Preparation: You will need to create a booklet out of construction paper, for each person. Use these colors: green, blue, red, brown, white, pink and orange. There will be one page of each color in each book. Take each piece of construction paper and fold it in fourths. Cut apart the paper into the four rectangles. The books will be this size. Punch a hole in the top corner of each page. Have colored yarn or string available for binding the book together. Have markers and stickers available for the study to decorate the pages.

How to implement this study: Lay out all the colored rectangles on the table. As each one assembles their Giving Thanks booklet (in the order of colors below), have them take a colored rectangle and write their thanks and decorate the page. After all the pages are complete, bind them together with the yarn. (option: you can assemble the books before you begin and just hand them out to be filled in.)

This study is going to teach us that we can offer thanks for the good in our lives and the not-so-good in our lives. Offering thanks to God is a command that brings a blessing to God and it also brings blessings to us. On each colored page of your booklet, you are going to be giving thanks for the good and the "bad" in your life. It's a sure cure for the blues!

GREEN – On the first green page, write a thanksgiving for something that is **GROWING** in your heart (for example, faith, trust, obedience, etc.) On the back of the green page, give thanks for something that is **GOING** out of your heart (for example, bad attitudes, fear, etc.).

BLUE – On the blue page, write a thanksgiving for a **BLESSING** in your life (a necessity in your life like a good family, a nice home, etc.) and on back of the blue page, give thanks for a **BLOOPER** in your life (a disappointment, a failure, etc.)

RED – Give thanks for something **REAL** in your life on the red page (an object – like clothes, a toy, etc.) and on the back of the red page give thanks for something **RIDICULOUS** (like your favorite candy, McDonalds, etc.).

Brown – Give thanks for some kind of **BONUS** in your life on the brown page (excellent vision, you run fast, etc.), then on the back of the brown page give thanks for **BUTTERFLIES** (something in your life that was really cool but now it's gone, like a vacation or a friend who moved, etc.)

White – On the white page, give thanks for a **WOW** (something that wows you, like a sunset or a rainbow), and on the back of the white page give thanks for a **WISH** that hasn't come true yet. (maybe you wish to grow tall, or you wish for a new puppy…)

Pink – Give thanks for a specific **PERSON** in your life on the pink page. (a teacher, a parent, etc.) On the back of the pink page give thanks for something that is a **PAIN** in your life (homework, chores, etc.).

Orange – Lastly, on the orange page, give thanks for something about the **OCEAN** (it's bigness, seashells, etc.). On the back of the orange page give thanks for something **OLD** (a favorite old blanket, a grandparent, etc.).

Notice all of the colors in your book:

1. There are two of each color, one with a thanksgiving for something "good" and one with a thanksgiving for something that might not seem to be good. The reason for the two being the same color is because in God's eyes, he makes all things work together for good in our lives. This is the reason we can give thanks for both, the good and the "bad". *(Read I Thessalonians 5:16-18)*.

2. Flip through your book. The colors are pretty. We can give thanks for everything because we know that God is in control and he makes all things beautiful and good. This doesn't mean everything that happens to us is going to look good to us. It does mean that everything that happens to us that is intended for evil will be turned around and be used for good. *(Read Romans 8:28)*.

3. Finally, have each one take turns reading each page of your book aloud, giving thanks to God for all things. Next time you feel blue – Take out this book and begin to thank God for all sorts of things. You might even want to add some pages. Soon you'll be smiling again…*(Read I Corinthians 15:56-58)*.

Christmas:

RECEIVE!

This study examines the wonderful gift God gave to us.

Preparation: You will need to place the following items in a box (shoebox size): bottle of water, small cups for each person, matches, a scented candle, piece of loaf bread and a pretty placemat). Then wrap the box with paper, tape and ribbon or a bow. Put a nametag on it with John 3:16 written inside.

How to implement this study: This study is to demonstrate the love of God in giving us the gift of life, and to get everyone to realize all we have to do is receive. As you examine the box, slowly open it up, talking about each part as indicated below. Then enjoy the feast inside, discussing the gift itself. Receive peace, joy and love from the giver of life.

Examine the gift:

The ***gift tag*** says who the gift is to: John 3:16 says the gift is for anyone who believes *(remove the gift tag.)*

The ***ribbon or bow*** decorates the package to make it pretty:

Isa. 61:10 says he clothes us with salvation and adorns (dresses) us like a bride with jewels. (*Take off the bow.*)

The _tape_ holds the paper on the box: Psalm 121:7,8 says he keeps watch over us all of our life, forever and ever. (*Tear the tape to open up the paper that covers the box.*)

The _paper_ itself covers the box: Psalm 32: 1,2 says our sins are covered and forgiven and not counted against us. (*Remove the paper.*)

The _box_ holds the gift: James 1:17 says every good and perfect gift is from above, coming down from the Father. He gave us the perfect gift, his son Jesus Christ. (Set the gift out in the middle of the group.)

Open the gift and receive:

(Have the kids open the gift and set out the things they find)

Jesus brings us living _water_ (John 4:10-13) – *pour everyone a cup and drink.*

He is the _bread_ of life (Eph. 2:8) – *share the bread and eat it.*

He gives us the gift of the _Holy Spirit_ (Acts 1:4,5) – *light the candle and breathe in it's fragrance.*

With this gift we receive peace, joy and love. This gift can be opened every day and enjoyed. It is up to us. Don't leave the gift sitting there, open it up and enjoy it!

- pray for one another to receive peace, joy and love -

Christmas:

Curiosity

This study teaches us how to use wisdom when we are "curious".

Preparation: You will need to wrap two gifts very differently. One gift will be empty, and the other will have the letter on the last page of this study folded neatly inside, plus a treat suited for each person participating (their favorite gum, candy or fruit). The empty box should be one from the trash, stuffed with dirty papers, wrapped in thin white tissue paper that is not even taped, just barely held together with ribbon, and a loose bow sitting on top. The box with the treats should be a nice box, lined with colorful tissue paper covering the gift, wrapped with extremely nice seasonal paper, with even edges, nicely taped, with ribbon and a colorful bow securely attached to the top. Finally, place a tag on the empty box, but don't write anything on it. On the other tag, write "my children" in the "to" space, and "your heavenly father" in the "from" space. You want both gifts to be attractive to the "eye", making those who look at them "curious" about what's inside.

How to implement this study: Sit around the tree or near some Christmas lights and have the two boxes in the center. Take turns being "curious" as you read the study and perform the tasks.

Curiosity - a desire to know more about something. Is this good? It can be. Is it bad? It can be.

Throughout your life, you will at times be curious. Curiosity gets little kids into trouble sometimes. If a child sees something on the floor, wonders what it is and picks it up and puts it in their mouth, this could be very dangerous. However, curiosity is something we all have, and it can be good if we are curious about the right things.

Look at these two gifts. Aren't you a little bit curious who they are for, who they are from and what's inside? Both gifts are wrapped and have a tag on them. Let's look a little closer and see how being curious might be a good thing, or it could be a bad thing…

Both gifts are attractive, right? Both have a pretty bow on top. (*Pick up the gifts and examine the bows. One of the bows should fall off.*) One bow was securely fastened to the package, and the other one fell right off! It wasn't even attached! The gifts we receive from God are secure. Our salvation is a beautiful thing, and it cannot be taken from us. However, anything Satan offers you will be a lie, and nothing he offers will be secure. (*Toss the loose bow aside.*)

Let's see who the gifts are for. (*Read the name tags on each gift.*) Wow, one is written personally and signed by God! However, the other tag is blank! That's curious. Why would someone take the time to wrap a gift and not sign the tag? Anything your heavenly father gives you is hand-picked just for you and he signs his name to it. Anything Satan sets before you is blank, just causing you to be curious enough to look, but he won't take credit for the gift, because his "gifts" are full of deceit, trickery and lies. Read II Corinthians 9:15. Begin to give thanks now for the gift, signed especially to you from your father. (*Take off the tags and lay them aside.*)

Notice the paper that was used in wrapping. (*Examine the differences in the paper.*) One package is wrapped with thick, colorful paper, in the colors of the season. The other gift is wrapped in thin, see-through tissue paper, with no color at all. God's gifts to us come at the right season of our life, and they are covered with his great love, goodness and mercy. Anything Satan tries to offer us will be flimsily wrapped, see-through and easily torn. Learn to recognize these differences when you are "curious" about things you see... Read James 1:16, 17.

Let's look further at the packages.

(*Notice how the gifts are wrapped.*) The nice paper is taped securely at all edges with nice clean lines, and all the corners are straight and neat. The person who gave us this gift must have really taken a lot of time and care in wrapping it! The other package isn't even taped at all. It looks like this gift took no time or thought to wrap! You're right. Satan doesn't care about you at all. He just throws things in your path to make you curious, but they are careless obstacles sent just to trip you. God's gifts to you are from his heart. (*Take off the paper from the boxes.*)

Take a look at the boxes. (*Examine the boxes.*) One box is nice. It looks like a box for a nice gift! I wonder what is inside??? Aren't you curious? The other box looks like it was taken right out of the trash can! Anything Satan offers you in life is from a trash heap. He only offers dirty, used-up ideas and tricks to place in your life. God's packages are made specifically for the gift inside, uniquely created for you and your life.

(*Open the boxes just enough to see the paper inside.*) Oh my, one is so beautiful. The tissue paper is soft and folded, and it looks so inviting! The other box is full of trashy wadded up paper that looks awful! If we examine closely, anything the world has to offer us will be covered with junk, and it's not worth picking your way through it to try and find something good. Who wants a piece of bread if they have to dig through a trash can to get it? God loves us. That's a fact. Look at the care and consideration he has given to present us with a gift designed especially for us. Feel the softness of the tissue paper. Look at the beautiful print. Why even be curious about the other package?

Finally, we get to the gift. (*Pull back the paper to reveal what's inside each box*). Inside every gift from God is something good, something just for us, something to bring him glory. Inside every "gift" we think we're receiving from the world around us is empty and shallow. <u>Read Ephesians 1:3-8.</u>

So is being curious a bad thing? No, but be wise when you are curious. Anything that looks good on the outside is not always good on the inside, and could even be harmful! Make sure that you are curious about God's love, his word, his wonders and his majesty, and you will be pleasantly surprised every time! (*Enjoy your treats.*)

Dear child of mine:

My gift to you this Christmas is the same as the gift I gave to the world over 2000 years ago. I came to give you life. I gave my life so that you might live. This gift is yours, free for the asking. I gladly laid down my life for you because I love you. I have always loved you and I always will.

The gift I give you goes on and on every day. It won't go out of style. It won't wear out. You will not get tired of it. It will satisfy your every desire. My love is enough to carry you throughout your entire life.

Reach out your hand and take mine, I will never let go. I loved you before you were born, I love you now and I <u>will always love you</u>.

Enjoy your treat while you sit at my feet.
Look at the lights and remember that night
Let me fill your desires while you sip by the fire
Enjoy this season for all the right reasons
Look at the tree and remember me.

Merry Christmas... ....Your heavenly Father

Christmas:

Celebrate!

In this study, we find the reasons for the season.

Preparation: You will need some blankets and candles, a tree branch for each person, bells or noisemakers of any kind, red lipstick, a dictionary a manger scene, and drums (you can use upside bowls and spoons).

How to implement this study: Make sure each one has a copy of this study with the words to the Christmas carols. As a family, you will be celebrating the birth of your savior, Jesus Christ.

Why do we celebrate the birth of Jesus at Christmas? What's the big deal? Let's look and see:

Read Matthew 1:17-21.
The birth of Jesus was a holy birth. He came to the earth to save us from our sins. He was pure, holy and without sin, the perfect sacrifice for our sins.

(Wrap yourselves in blankets, light the candles and sing "Silent Night").

> Silent night, holy night
> All is calm, all is bright
> Round yon Virgin Mother and Child
> Holy Infant so tender and mild
> Sleep in heavenly peace
> Sleep in heavenly peace

Read Luke 2:13, 14.
The angels praised God for sending his son, Jesus. It was a joyous time to celebrate the birth of the savior of the world. That's why we praise him too, because he is the one who is worthy to be praised, the savior of our soul!

(Wave your branch as you sing).

> Joy to the world, the Lord is come!
> Let earth receive her King;
> Let every heart prepare Him room,
> And Heaven and nature sing,
> And Heaven and nature sing,
> And Heaven, and Heaven, and nature sing

Read Matthew 2:9, 10
Jesus brings laughter and joy to those who take a ride with him through life.

(Ring your bells as you sing with joy).

> Dashing through the snow
> In a one horse open sleigh
> O'er the fields we go
> Laughing all the way
> Bells on bob tails ring
> Making spirits bright
> What fun it is to laugh and sing

A sleighing song tonight
Oh, jingle bells, jingle bells
Jingle all the way
Oh, what fun it is to ride
In a one horse open sleigh
Jingle bells, jingle bells
Jingle all the way
Oh, what fun it is to ride
In a one horse open sleigh

Read John 8:3-11.
Rudolph was an outcast among the reindeer because he was odd. In this story we read of a lady who was an outcast because of her sin. However, this story shows the kind of love Jesus has for the sinner, even when other around point the finger and accuse.

(Paint your noses red (with the lipstick), and sing this song for all the outcasts of society, praying that Jesus will call them by name and give them a place of honor in his kingdom.)

Rudolph, the red-nosed reindeer
had a very shiny nose.
And if you ever saw him,
you would even say it glows.

All of the other reindeer
used to laugh and call him names.
They never let poor Rudolph
join in any reindeer games.

Then one foggy Christmas Eve
Santa came to say:

"Rudolph with your nose so bright,
won't you guide my sleigh tonight?"
Then all the reindeer loved him
as they shouted out with glee,
Rudolph the red-nosed reindeer,
you'll go down in history!

(Use your dictionary to look up these words, then sing the carol: Hark, herald, reconciled, host)

Hark! The herald angels sing
"Glory to the newborn King!
Peace on earth and mercy mild
God and sinners reconciled"
Joyful, all ye nations rise
Join the triumph of the skies
With angelic host proclaim:
"Christ is born in Bethlehem"
Hark! The herald angels sing
"Glory to the newborn King!"

Read Luke 2:8-12.
The manger scene shows a great story, God came to earth to save sinners like you and I, he is worthy to be praised, he brings peace to all who know him and it's a joyful event, a time to celebrate and give glory to his name.

(Set up the manger scene, as you sing this carol).

O Come All Ye Faithful
Joyful and triumphant,
O come ye, O come ye to Bethlehem.
Come and behold Him,
Born the King of Angels;
O come, let us adore Him,
O come, let us adore Him,
O come, let us adore Him,
Christ the Lord.

Read Luke 6:38. Christmas is all about giving. Christ was given to us, we are to give back to him. Give to him freely and you will be blessed. The little drummer boy had no gifts to bring. However, he played the drums, using a talent he had. We all have been given talents and when we use them for His glory, he is pleased.

(Sing this carol and play your "drums").

Come they told me, pa rum pum pum pum
A new born King to see, pa rum pum pum pum
Our finest gifts we bring, pa rum pum pum pum
To lay before the King, pa rum pum pum pum,
rum pum pum pum, rum pum pum pum,

So to honor Him, pa rum pum pum pum,
When we come.

Little Baby, pa rum pum pum pum
I am a poor boy too, pa rum pum pum pum
I have no gift to bring, pa rum pum pum pum
That's fit to give the King, pa rum pum pum pum,
rum pum pum pum, rum pum pum pum,

Shall I play for you, pa rum pum pum pum,
On my drum?

Mary nodded, pa rum pum pum pum
The ox and lamb kept time, pa rum pum pum pum
I played my drum for Him, pa rum pum pum pum
I played my best for Him, pa rum pum pum pum,
rum pum pum pum, rum pum pum pum,

Then He smiled at me, pa rum pum pum pum
Me and my drum.

Enjoy the Christmas season and Celebrate the birth of Christ!

To learn more about Ambassador International and view our catalog of products, log on to our Web site:
www.emeraldhouse.com